From
Rags to Riches

From
Rags to Riches

A STORY OF ABU DHABI

Mohammed Al Fahim

The London Centre of Arab Studies

Copyright © 1995 Mohammed Al Fahim

First published 1995 by London Center of Arab Studies Ltd.
Vicarage House
58-60 Kensington Church Street
London W8 4DB

This new edition 2007 published by Makarem G Trading and Real Estate LLC
Abu Dhabi, United Arab Emirates

British Library Cataloguing-in-Publication Data.
A Catalogue record for this book is available
from the British Library

ISBN 1 900404 00 1

Printed and bound in Dubai

To Sheikh Zayed bin Sultan Al Nahyan; to my father, Abduljalil Al Fahim, and to all the children of the United Arab Emirates.

ACKNOWLEDGEMENTS

I could not have written this book without the help of a talented wordsmith. My sincerest thanks to Susan Macaulay who transformed my thoughts and ideas into a polished product of which we can both be very proud. Her patience, persistence and probing questions focused our energies as we wrote and edited the manuscript; her journalistic skills enlivened the stories appearing on the pages that follow. *From Rags to Riches* is as much a credit to her expertise as it is a result of my determined research over several years.

I also received support from many others, all of whom I would like to thank for their much-appreciated advice, encouragement and help:

Dr. Mohammed Morsy Abdullah, Director of the Centre for Documentation and Research of the UAE, an authority on the history of the Gulf region and author of the book *The United Arab Emirates: A Modern History*, for his advice, assistance and encouragement. His wealth of knowledge and his insightful comments were of infinite benefit.

Mary Bouery, my personal assistant for more than ten years, for her support in all my work as well as this important project.

Jane Priestland for her help in gathering the background information that formed the foundation for the book.

A nameless friend whose encouragement, support and enthusiasm enlightened my thoughts thus ensuring me success in this endeavour.

My uncles Ahmed and Abdul Rahim Al Fahim, to whom I turned on countless occasions for clarification and relevant historical background: they made my research as enjoyable as it was fascinating.

For the photographs, reproduced by courtesy of; Abu Dhabi Company for Onshore Oil Operations (ADCO); The British Petroleum Company (BP); Curtis Brown on behalf of Wilfred Thesiger © W. Thesiger.

Special thanks to my family, particularly my daughters Shereen, Maha, Hanadi and Reem whose incisive comments and critiques were too important to ignore. Heartfelt gratitude to my wife who shouldered the burden of looking after our children during the two summers I pored over research material and read a huge number of historical books on the Emirates. Thanks also to my sons Khalid, Ahmed and Rashid who kept their noisy battery-powered toys away from my study as I worked and who sincerely believed that Susan was my teacher from the way she carried her reference books.

CONTENTS

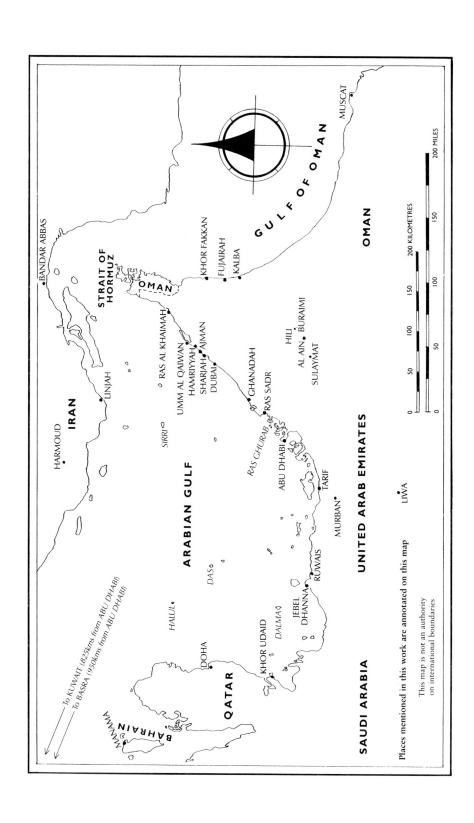

Foreword

A year ago, Mohammed bin Abdul Jalil Al Fahim visited the Centre for Documentation and Research in Abu Dhabi asking for documents to read on the contemporary history of his country. I have known Mohammed since my arrival in Abu Dhabi in 1968 and have followed his career with admiration and respect. He worked for many years for his father, with whom he shared his ambitions in developing his country. Some years ago, Mohammed, as a result of his achievements and experiences, was elected as deputy chairman of the Chamber of Commerce and Industry in Abu Dhabi.

Mohammed's interest in the history of his country's development led him to consult not only those documents held at the Centre in Abu Dhabi, but also the papers of the Foreign Office Archives in London. As a historian, I was keen that Mohammed should write his own memoirs. They would record the experiences of a child growing up in an impoverished society who watches its transformation, almost overnight, into one with unimaginable wealth and technology at its disposal.

His story describes the life of a strong, influential Arab family, forced by Iranian expansion to emigrate from Hurmoud, in Southern Iran, to Dubai to Dalma Island, Abu Dhabi and then to Al Ain in the heart of the desert. His grandfather married a woman from the Hawamil, a branch of the Bani Yas Federation in Abu Dhabi.

The early part of Mohammed's book deals with major developments in the Gulf States and the daily life and events of the Gulf Arabs during the late nineteenth century and the early part of the twentieth century. He relates his family's history with stories handed down by his grandfather and father. The book tells of the close friendship between his father and Sheikh Zayed bin Sultan. Mohammed spent much of his childhood in Sheikh Zayed's palace and became acquainted with the leading members of the ruling family and other influential personalities of the country which has helped to make his book an important primary source of information.

Mohammed was an eyewitness to many important recent developments. His own experiences during his successful career in the private sector, his travels and knowledge of regional and international economies have added to the significance of his writing. Although Mohammed is not a writer by profession, his skill and sensitivity in presenting his memoirs qualify him to be added to the list of gifted writers in the Emirates today. His work has value in its truthful simplicity and describes events in the 1930s and 1940s with frankness, events which many people with his background and experiences would prefer to forget. Many histories of the Emirates have been written in recent years, but Mohammed's story differs from a conventional history of the area in that it deals with the personal story of a knowledgeable citizen growing up with loneliness due to the tragic deaths of both his mother and his sister, yet with the Muslims' faith, trust and acceptance of the will of God. Mohammed's story is one of courage and determination, told with honesty and humour. I hope that his book will encourage other leading men and women who have made significant contributions to the recent history of the United Arab Emirates to write their memoirs.

Dr. M. Morsy Abdullah
Director Centre for Documentation & Research
Cultural Foundation, Abu Dhabi.

Introduction

The peoples of the Arabian Peninsula have long been blessed with a rich oral tradition through which knowledge, experience and wisdom are passed from one generation to the next. Many of the important events of our history are not recorded anywhere but in the memories of our people. They live on in the stories, myths and legends that our sons and daughters are told by senior family members. Woven together, these stories form the colourful tapestry of our past.

I have always been fascinated by the tales my father and uncles told of the trials and tribulations as well as the joys and triumphs of their lives. As their stories were recounted to me I relived some of their experiences in my imagination and developed a deep interest in the history of my people. However, as I read more books on the history of the Emirates, I failed to find anything that compared with the stories I had been told by my family. While there were factual historical accounts of events, there seemed to be little written of the people of Abu Dhabi, their heroic struggles against the elements, hunger, poverty and deprivation or their fierce determination to overcome adversity. At the same time I noticed that the storytelling traditions which have been part of our lives for generations have now begun to take a back seat to more modern, though far less interesting, channels of communication. I felt we were in danger of losing an important era in our history simply because it might slip away with the passing of the generation preceding my own, so I decided to document some of our recent history myself.

As an eyewitness to the 1950s, 60s and 70s, I felt it was my duty to record and pass on some of the important events of those years to the younger generations and to enlighten newcomers to the United Arab Emirates generally, and to Abu Dhabi in particular, as to what life was like here before the discovery of oil. The changes that have taken place throughout the Emirates over the past three decades have been incredible, difficult to believe even for those who have seen them with their own eyes. Less than fifty years ago our lives hung in the balance almost daily. We placed ourselves in God's hands, praying for protection. In fact, I might not have been here today to write this book had it not been for God's grace protecting me when I was little more than a toddler.

During a trip across the desert to Al Ain from Abu Dhabi in 1950, my mother cradled me in her arms as she rode a camel through the dunes in the hot sun. The seven-day trek was strenuous and tiring and my mother dozed off from exhaustion. I slipped from her arms, became entangled in her dress and dangled on the side of the camel for quite some time before an aunt who was riding ahead turned back to see me suspended, swinging back and forth with the camel's gait. The caravan stopped, I was rescued and all thanked God I had been saved. Today, my own children sleep in the comfort of air conditioning whenever we make the two-hour trip between Abu Dhabi and Al Ain. Times have changed.

Nearly fifteen years after I had hung helplessly from the side of that camel, building had begun in Abu Dhabi. At the time the island sand was used to make the concrete that went into everything that was being constructed. Our teacher told us then that a day would come when there would not be enough sand in Abu Dhabi to build all the roads, houses and buildings we would need for our city. We scoffed at this impossibility. We had enough sand in Abu Dhabi to last until forever and beyond. Less than five years later the impossible became a reality when we had to bring in sand from the desert to meet our construction needs.

When I requested permission from Sheikh Zayed to write about his journey through the troubled waters of the past with the people of Abu Dhabi, he gave his assent gladly, telling me it is crucial for us to cherish yesterday if we are to be successful in conquering tomorrow. Though he lives in luxury now, he has never forgotten the difficult years of his life. It is vital that we follow his example by remembering the lessons of the past as well as the courage of our ancestors.

I am not a historian. Nor am I a writer by profession. My intention in putting this book together was not to create a historical or literary masterpiece. Rather, it was to highlight, through simple stories, the important events that shaped our future by changing our society from that of the nomadic bedouin to one that is progressive, organised and equipped with all the tools required to make the most of the modern world. I have told the stories from my own perspective, which may in some cases differ from that of others who have studied and commented on our history before me. This is only natural. I refer in particular to how distinctly differently I, as a UAE national, may view our history compared with, for example, how a British subject might see it. This does not mean to say that I hold the present British government, or indeed its citizens, responsible for the events that took place here in the Gulf from the beginning of the

1800s until we achieved independence in 1971. What happened then is now water under the bridge and we must continue working toward a more balanced and mutually beneficial relationship on both sides.

I took up the challenge of writing this book for the sake of the next generation of UAE nationals so that they might know of the hardships we suffered before Sheikh Zayed put the oil revenues to work for all our people. My sincere hope is that our children will find enlightenment as well as some lessons hidden within the pages that follow and that they will put them to good use as they strive to make their dreams come true.

Mohammed Al Fahim
Abu Dhabi
1995.

Chapter 1

Humble Beginnings

The Trucial States

Today, the United Arab Emirates comprises seven emirates – Abu Dhabi, Dubai, Sharjah, Ras al Khaimah, Umm al Qaiwain, Fujairah and Ajman – occupying a total area of about 77,700 square kilometres, similar to that of Scotland. The UAE is bordered by much larger neighbours – Qatar and Saudi Arabia to the west and south and Oman to the east – and is separated from Iran by the expanse of the Arabian Gulf. Its total population was estimated at close to one and a half million in the early 1990s. However, only one-third of its residents are UAE nationals; the balance comprises expatriate workers, primarily Muslims from other Arab countries, Iran and Asia.

Despite its small size and population the UAE has become more known worldwide over the last two decades, owing in large part to its abundance of oil reserves and the role it consequently has to play in the world's energy markets. Before 1971, however, the situation was vastly different. Not only did the UAE not exist as a country on any world map, its history, culture and people were unknown to all but a select few who had come to visit its sandy shores. It did not even have a proper name...

The local people had called it the coast of Oman up until the 1950s. In the late eighteenth and early nineteenth centuries the British called it the "Pirate Coast", but after the conclusion of the perpetual truce agreements of 1853 they called it the "Trucial Coast," or "Trucial States." For simplicity's sake, I shall refer to it as the Trucial States as I recount some of the stories of its people and its history.

While there has been no reliable census information available for the Gulf region until very recently, the indigenous population of the Trucial States in the early 1800s was probably around 72,000.[1] Small villages dotted the coast at Ras al Khaimah, Sharjah, Dubai and Abu Dhabi. They were inhabited mainly by fishermen, pearl divers, seafarers and their families who depended almost exclusively on the sea for their livelihood. Other than activities related directly to

[1]*Lorimer, pg 1437 (Vol II B)*

maritime enterprises, such as boat building and supply services for the seasonal pearl diving, there was virtually no industry.

Similarly, the inland territories had little to offer. There was some agricultural activity in Ras Al Khaimah, Fujairah and parts of Khorfakkan and Kalba, and at the oases of Liwa and Al Ain in the territory of Abu Dhabi. Locally-grown dates were the main staple food. However, local production could not feed even the small population of the time so people relied on imports from Basrah, Iraq and Bahrain to supplement what was cultivated in the area. The local diet also included camel milk, upon which the bedouin depended heavily, and fish which was eaten mostly by the coastal people as it perished in less than a day in the heat.

They traded pearls in exchange for basic necessities. Almost everything - from foodstuffs to cloth - had to be imported, some items from as far afield as East Africa and India although trade was brisk with closer neighbours as well. Because of their proximity, towns and villages on the southern coast of Persia - Bandar-Abbas, Linjah and later Bushire, for example - were all active trading partners. Most of the settlements on the Persian coast, as well as many of the islands which lay between Abu Dhabi and Persia, were controlled by the Al Qawasim of Ras Al Khaimah. Their sheikhdom, which stretched from Abu Dhabi, across the Strait of Hormuz and along the southern coast of Persia, was inhabited mainly by Arabs from the Al Ali tribe as well as other smaller tribes of Arabic origin.

The political system of the time was centred in the tribal chiefs, also known as rulers or sheikhs. The ruling sheikh was the all-powerful governor of his people, overseeing everything associated with their well-being and prosperity. He judged disputes between tribes and individuals; imposed fines or imprisonment; maintained the government coffers and treasury; declared war and negotiated peace; supported the inland tribes with available finances and food supplies; levied taxes and tariffs; received foreign representatives and signed agreements on behalf of his people. He also charged taxes on pearl diving boats and in most cases owned several such vessels himself.

At the beginning of the nineteenth century the Trucial States comprised three sheikhdoms, Abu Dhabi, Ras al Khaimah and Sharjah, each of which had its own ruling sheikh. Ideally, a sheikh governed in consultation with the elders and prominent members of the tribe, village, or town. In reality, however, the sheikhs made most decisions on their own with limited input from others. This system of tribal government, which had existed in the Gulf for centuries, survived in the area of the Trucial States until the 1960s.

As they still do now, most of the inhabitants of the Trucial States belonged to the Sunni sect of Islam. They had been Muslim ever since the Islamic movement swept across the Arabian Peninsula and Iran in the seventh century AD.

Also just as it is today, the Sheikhdom of Abu Dhabi was the largest of the sheikhdoms in the area known as the Trucial States. Its territory was bordered to the east by Dubai (which was part of Abu Dhabi until 1833), to the west by Qatar and present-day Saudi Arabia, and to the south by the Sultanate of Oman. Within Abu Dhabi's territory there were three main settled areas: the five-mile-wide by six-mile-long island of Abu Dhabi and the oases of Al Ain and the Liwa. Like other inhabitants of the Trucial States, the people of Abu Dhabi led a very simple, almost primitive, existence throughout the eighteenth, nineteenth and most of the twentieth centuries. Where the city of Abu Dhabi stands today there had been only a sparsely populated seasonal settlement for several hundred years. Some people wintered here, or came in the spring to prepare for the pearling season, but the village was virtually deserted for the hot summers until a permanent town was established in the 1960s. Most of the people who lived in Abu Dhabi during the winter spent their summers either in the Liwa or Al Ain where there was fresh water and shade from the sun. In addition to the relatively sedentary populations dwelling primarily in the three settled areas, Abu Dhabi was also home to several nomadic bedouin tribes who lived in the desert surviving on the little their habitat had to offer. Both the nomads and the settled people, all belonging to the Bani Yas tribes, lived much as their forefathers had for several generations: the former practised animal husbandry, the latter derived their very modest incomes almost exclusively from pearl diving.

Pearling - bitter memories
Pearls have been treasured and traded as beautiful adornments for the wealthy for centuries, and, until the 1950s, the Gulf was one of the most prolific pearl producing areas in the world. In fact it was pearls which initially attracted foreign traders to the area, Portuguese invaders in the early sixteenth century and Indian merchants from the seventeenth century onwards. Pearling began in this region some two thousand years ago, when boats were first used to ferry people across the Gulf. By the nineteenth century it had become the lifeblood of the people who lived in these harshly beautiful yet unforgiving lands. Although the fruits of their labour were exquisite, the conditions under which the pearl divers worked were abominable and it was with considerable dread that Abu Dhabians anticipated the onset of each pearling season.

Like many other resource-based industries pearl diving was a seasonal activity, one best suited to the summer months in the Gulf. The warmer water was conducive to diving and less attractive to sharks as well as other large fish which prefer the cooler temperatures prevailing along the coast in winter. At the end of the 19th century Abu Dhabi had the largest pearling fleet - over 400 boats - in the Trucial States. It was followed by Sharjah (360). Dubai (335), Umm al Qaiwain (70), Ras al Khaimah (57) and Ajman (40). The fleets set out in May or June and did not return until September when the season was over. The pearlers - divers and their helpers - were separated from their families for the duration of the three to four month long season despite the fact that they were often within fifty kilometres of mainland Abu Dhabi. The captains and ship owners were loath to bring them back and thus lose even a day or two of diving for the sake of a family visit.

If they did return at all it was to take up arms for the ruling sheikh. The pearl divers and seamen fought hand-to-hand when the ruler called for an invasion of a neighbouring territory or when he needed to defend his own territory against an aggressor. Every now and then the season was disrupted by these calls to arms. When conflicts escalated the divers' season was shortened, their income declined accordingly and they had a more difficult time making ends meet. Nevertheless, war and poverty may have been easier to deal with than life aboard the pearling vessels.

The boats were small, particularly after 1820 when the British limited the size of vessels which could be built in the Trucial States. They could comfortably carry six or seven people. When they set out for the season, however, they were overloaded with as many as twenty-seven men plus enough provisions to last until the first supply boat met them at sea several weeks later. The boats were so overcrowded with equipment, diving gear, food supplies and water that there was hardly room for the men to sit, let alone sleep at night. During the day the sun beat down on them mercilessly, making the already unbearable heat and humidity even more hellish.

The days were long and arduous. Divers were in the water just after dawn and often stayed there until twelve hours later when the light began to fade. They dived constantly throughout the day, only stopping, literally, to catch their breath. A diver's equipment included a bag in which to gather the oysters, a goat horn clip to close his nose and a rope tied around his waist by which a partner on the boat pulled him up at the end of each dive. The dives lasted for about two minutes each - time enough to pluck a dozen or so oysters from the sandbank some twenty metres below. They paused for only a minute between each two minute dive, resting a little longer after every tenth trip to the bottom.

These long stretches in the salty depths caused debilitating and dangerous muscle cramps as well as painful skin and eye diseases for which the only available treatments at the time were herbal medicines. If a diver surfaced too quickly he risked damaging his ears or his brain, too slowly and he risked death by drowning. In addition, there was always the danger of predatory fish including sharks which were known to stray close to the coast despite their preference for cooler waters.

If the day's take was plentiful the men were sometimes made to open the oysters in the evening to look for the pearls hidden inside even though they had already put in a full day of diving. Any oysters which had not been broken open in the evening were searched the next morning before the men began diving for the day. They normally ate only in the evening because it was impossible to dive on a full stomach. Many men lost all their teeth as a result of being undernourished – they survived primarily on small rations of dates, rice and fish for the duration of the season. Fresh water was supplied irregularly, if at all, and more often than not the drinking water was either brackish or drawn from rusty barrels in which it had been transported from shore to the fleet. On top of all this the elements played cruel tricks: sometimes the wind blew so hard they were prevented from diving; at other times they were becalmed, forcing the men, already tired and overworked, to row the heavy boats from one location to another. It was exhausting work that wore down even the toughest among them but if they slowed down, fell ill or wanted to rest the captains sometimes punished them with a beating or reduced their share of the season's income.

Day in and day out for three months they worked long hours under deplorable conditions – conditions which may have been more easily endured had there at least been reasonable financial rewards. But the boats rarely returned with sufficient pearls to pay the debts of all those aboard and still make a small profit. In fact the men and their families often slipped into a spiralling circle of debt from which there was little hope of escape.

In the spring they borrowed against the upcoming season to pay for their provisions and provide for their families while they were away. They were only paid when the season was over and the pearls had been sold or traded to the merchants who would export them to India for distribution and resale. Ten per cent of the season's take went to the ship owner and another twenty per cent paid for the supplies. The remaining seventy per cent was divided between the captain, who received three shares, the divers and helpers each of whom received one share, and the ruling sheikh who also received the equivalent of one diver's share from each boat in the fleet. When all was said and done the divers ended up with little, if anything.

Besides the poverty the men were plagued with ill health. They came back from the diving expeditions sick and undernourished, often suffering from scurvy or skin afflictions and completely worn out. It took them three to five months to recover from the three month season. The diving also deprived children of their youth. Boys started diving at the age of twelve to supplement their family's income. Like the other divers the youngsters had to dive long and deep despite the fact that it was an even greater strain on their still-developing lungs and respiratory systems.

By the latter part of the 1800s better diving technology and equipment had been developed. These more advanced technologies, which were in use in the Mediterranean, the sea of Japan and the Far East, could easily have lessened the hardships suffered by the divers here. However, the British prevented the importation of new equipment into the Gulf, partly from self interest, partly because they wanted the pearling industry to remain in Arab hands. Furthermore, steam-powered ships which began appearing in the Gulf in the 1860s were never available to the pearlers here; they were still using wind- and man-powered vessels when the industry began to decline in the 1930s. It was a difficult life with few rewards.

In rare cases the divers were compensated handsomely for a particularly large and lustrous pearl, but the majority could hardly make ends meet let alone pay off their loans. Most of what they earned went to repay the debts they had incurred with the merchants and suppliers before they left. Sometimes they even came back empty-handed despite having been out at sea for several months. When that happened they went even further into debt, compelling them to return to sea the following season in an effort to repay the increasing amounts they owed. It was a life of slavery. The people of Abu Dhabi, however, had little choice - pearling was their only source of income, the only way they could feed their families. So, by necessity, most led simple humble lives with few comforts and little hope for the future.

Bare essentials

With the exception of a few prominent merchants and the ruling family who had homes made of earth or clay, the majority lived in barasti houses fashioned from the large leafy branches of the date palm trees. This type of housing was used until the late 1960s when Sheikh Zayed became the ruler and city planning began in Abu Dhabi. Of course there were no modern amenities such as water or electricity. People used wood, brought in on the back of camels by the bedouin, as fuel for their cooking fires. The Al Ain and Liwa areas had ample supplies of fresh water. In Abu Dhabi, however, brackish water for drinking, cooking or bathing was drawn either from shallow wells dug within the confines of the house or its enclosure, or hauled from deeper communal wells located at some distance from the settlement. The water, although filtered through the sand and not quite as salty as the sea, was still sea water and not pure or clean like today's drinking water. Nevertheless, people had to drink it as there was no other alternative. In fact, the people of Abu Dhabi drank brackish water, drawn from their wells, until the first desalination plant began producing fresh water in 1961.

Naturally, there was no domestic help as there is today. Everyone – men, women and children – worked hard to eke out a living in the harsh, hot and humid environment of the Gulf coast and the barren inland desert. The women were in charge of the household. They cooked, cleaned, washed and cared for the children. Those who were married to fishermen sold the daily catch in the market. The fishermen brought their haul back to the island early in the morning and their wives took it to market to sell or exchange for other foodstuffs and household necessities. There were no schools for the children. Instead of being educated they began to work as soon as they were able. When they neared their teens the boys joined their fathers on the pearling or fishing boats and the additional income they earned went towards supporting the family.

Most people were too poor to protect themselves properly from the ravages of the elements: a simple cloth wrapped around the midriff left the men naked and vulnerable from the waist up. They had no shoes or head coverings and the majority, particularly the bedouin, wore their hair long to shield their necks from the burning rays of the sun, a style which changed only in the 1960s with the adoption of the gutra and agal as the national headdress.

A traveller who visited the area in the late 1800s had this to say of the local dress: "the inhabitants walk around with a piece of cloth around their waist, naked from the waist up with no shoes and nothing to cover their heads, armed with a spear, a sword or an antiquated gun."

Travel, especially over long distances, was a slow and tedious affair because it was on camel back. It took seven days to travel between Abu Dhabi and Al Ain, a distance of 160 kilometres, and five days to the Liwa. When travelling to the Liwa, some people went part way by boat before going overland from the sea shore (usually from a point somewhere near Ruwais) but it still took a full five days to reach their destination.

Unfortunately the routes were not without hazards – travellers were often harassed by bandits and robbers. Since it was dangerous to journey alone, families often travelled together in caravans for safety. The caravans usually left once or twice a month at the discretion of the camel owners who preferred to make the long treks relatively infrequently. The camels normally belonged to the bedouin tribes who tended and reared them in the desert where the occasional rainfall produced suitable fodder for the animals. The tribes moved with the camels from one grazing site to another throughout the year sometimes visiting the seaside with supplies of wood, dates or other essentials required by the inhabitants of the coastal settlements. The desert dwellers also offered protection to travellers through a code of hospitality they had practiced for generations.

Bedouin hospitality - timeless traditions

It was normal for caravans travelling between Abu Dhabi and Al Ain to come upon one or more bedouin encampments along the way. If the travellers were welcomed into the encampment, the bedouin hosts were obliged to protect the caravan for varying lengths of time depending on the type of hospitality supplied. An offer of coffee meant their safety then became the responsibility of the bedouin until the caravan was out of sight of the encampment. If the travellers stayed for a meal, their safety was guaranteed for the time it took a camel to journey one day. If, on the other hand, the travellers stayed overnight, they became the bedouin's responsibility for three days' journey from the encampment. If the caravans were attacked or molested in any way those who had offered hospitality were responsible for avenging the attack. Travellers took refuge in the desert through this system of hospitality. In return for protection they might give the bedouin food or purchase supplies or handicrafts from them.

Friendship also played a big role. In those days, the population was so small everyone knew each other. Before you neared an encampment they could tell from a distance who you were. If a foe approached he would not be allowed in the encampment; a traveller would never be offered coffee by the bedouin until they were sure they wanted to welcome him into their camp.

Traditions such as these were the basis of everyday life less than fifty years ago. People lived by them, and sought understanding of the world through them. The social conventions and customs governing the lives of the bedouin dictated certain codes of hospitality which, on the one hand, helped them distinguish friend from foe, and on the other, protected travellers from some of the dangers of a desert journey. Each tribe had unique traditions and customs practised by its members alone. People were able to recognise the subtle differences existing between various tribes and thus determine their relationship with one another. The customs were tools of communication, signs of understanding which guided their behaviour. If, for example, someone visited another's house and was not offered a refreshment, it was a clear sign of the host's displeasure with the visitor and an indication that he was not welcome. If coffee was withheld it meant the host was annoyed with the visitor. Similarly, if the guest did not drink the refreshment he was offered it was an indication that he was displeased with the host. In either case, a discussion would have to ensue following which the offer or acceptance of coffee, depending on who was displeased with whom, would indicate that the disagreement had been resolved.

These traditions live on to this day in Abu Dhabi and throughout the UAE. When a guest visits someone in his house or office, the guest is not really welcome until the host offers him coffee, tea or a soft drink as a sign of hospitality. Once the host has done so, however, the guest is free to state his business, problem or need and the host has the responsibility to listen to whatever business his guest wishes to discuss – in supplying the refreshment he has welcomed the guest and taken responsibility for the visit.

Unwanted domination

Few in number and leading simple lives within a political system under which they had existed for centuries, the inhabitants of the area had no desire to become involved with a dominating colonial power such as England. The British presence in the Gulf had first begun when the East India Company fleet helped Shah Abbas of Persia to expel the Portuguese from Hormuz in 1622. A year after the defeat of the Portuguese, the British established a commercial post at Bandar-Abbas; it was followed by similar installations at Isphahan, Shiraz and Basrah. From then on, their influence, trade and commercial activities grew in the region.

The Gulf remained relatively peaceful until the latter part of the next century when events occurring half a world away interrupted the calm: the war in which England and France were engaged spilled over into the Indian Ocean and beyond. It had a deep and long lasting impact on our development.

England was jealously guarding her interests in India. The French, however, were trying to further their own colonial goals by establishing a trading post in the Indian Ocean where they could resupply their ships and strengthen trade links with the Far East. They finally built a base at Ile de France, on Reunion Island, from which they began interfering with British ships – so-called acts of piracy which began to occur in the Gulf region as well, although here they were blamed exclusively, and many times erroneously, on the local

Arab seafarers. The French navy also bombarded and destroyed the English post at Bandar-Abbas in 1759, forcing them to relocate to Bushire where they established a new centre from which to supervise their commercial activities in the area.

With the French firmly rooted at Ile de France and challenging their position here, the British, who handled their trade in the region through the powerful East India Company, began searching for new markets and faster routes to key trading centres in Europe. One of the potential routes extended from India through the Gulf into Basrah, in Iraq, and overland from there up to Syria or Haifa, in what is now Israel, and across the Mediterranean to England. It was a shorter route from England to India than going around the Cape of Good Hope, a perilous journey which took months at that time. Despite the fact that the Ottomans dominated most of the region including Basrah, present-day Saudia Arabia, Kuwait and Bahrain, the British began strengthening their trade routes through the Gulf.

As they did so, it was inevitable that they should run into the Al Qawasim of Ras Al Khaimah, the most powerful tribe in the Trucial States at the time.

The Bani Yas and the Qawasim

During the eighteenth century, two tribal federations had emerged in the area that was to become known as the Trucial States. The first was the Bani Yas federation comprising a number of tribes led by the Al Falah family. Their seat of government was in the interior at the Liwa oasis which they shared with the Manasir and Mazari tribes.

However, when Sheikh Shakhbut bin Dyab came into power in 1793, he moved the base of the Bani Yas to the port of Abu Dhabi. He built a fort on the island and later extended his authority to the Al Ain oasis. Despite their new coastal "capital," the power of the Bani Yas tribes lay in their bedouin roots. Their heroic resistance against the Saudi expeditions to Buraimi, which was claimed by both Muscat and the Saudis, helped build strong long term relations between the Bani Yas and the Sultans of Muscat.

The second major tribal federation was the Qawasim. They controlled, until the late 1800s, most of what is now called the northern emirates, as well as the entrance to the Gulf and many of the towns on the Persian coast. Since the Qawasim's strength lay in their maritime and trading activities, they often found themselves in commercial rivalry with the Al Bu Said who ruled Muscat and the British for whom the Gulf area was becoming increasingly important.

During the latter part of the century the Qawasim embraced Wahhabism, a religious movement which, though based in Nejd, was expanding from its eastern borders through Bahrain and down the Gulf. The movement sought to free the holy places of Mecca and Medina from the control of the Ottoman empire and to spread the religious beliefs of Abdul-Wahhab, a conservative Islamic cleric who advocated strict adherence to the text of the Quran and considered all non-Muslims to be heathens. These teachings added fuel to the trade fires already smouldering between the Qawasim and the British, escalating tensions over the next decade. During that time, with the support of the Wahhabis, the Qawasim tried to protect their long-established trading interests from foreign interference. Inflamed by religious zeal and their commercial rivalry with the British and Omanis, they began attacking East India Company ships in the Gulf.

Both sides sustained substantial losses but, in 1819, a crushing blow devastated the Qawasim. Without so much as a warning, let alone a declaration of war, the British naval force in the Gulf raided the Port of Ras Al Khaimah destroying every ship that lay at anchor. Over 300 vessels of between 500 and 1,000 tonnes - the entire Qawasim fleet - was destroyed in a bombardment that is said to have lasted several days. Leaving this devastation behind the British fleet sailed down the Gulf and, over the next few days, destroyed the small ports and sailing vessels at Umm al Qaiwain and Ajman. Thankfully the Ports of Dubai and Abu Dhabi were spared as they had not been involved in any of the conflicts leading up to the bombardments. With this series of incidents the British presence in the Gulf - which had been primarily commercial until then - became distinctly military and political in nature.

The people of the Trucial States, disorganised as a result of inter-tribal conflicts and ill-equipped to repel an outside threat, had neither the capabilities nor the strength to fight it out with the British who were far superior to them in arms, men and equipment. The loss of their ships devastated the settlements along the coast. The inhabitants were no longer able to trade with neighbouring islanders and were thus robbed of a significant portion of their livelihood. They then had to rely more heavily on pearling - an arduous activity with meagre returns - to make a living.

The destruction of their fleet was also the beginning of the end of the Qawasim era in the region. Without ships to protect their interests, maintain their trade links, and conduct business, they began losing their territories on the Persian side of the Gulf in the second half of the nineteenth century.

General Keir, the leader of the British expedition against the Qawasim in 1819, insisted on concluding peace agreements with every sheikh in the area. As the supreme Sheikh of the Qawasim, Sheikh Sultan Bin Saqr had the power to sign an agreement on behalf of all the sheikhs within his dominion. He protested against Keir's insistence on concluding agreements with the sheikhs of Ajman and Umm al Qaiwain who had previously been under his authority. Sheikh Sultan's protestations fell on deaf ears, and from that point onwards the Sheikhdoms of Ajman and Umm al Qaiwain became independent of Ras al Khaimah, the seat of power of the Qawasim.

The split within the Qawasim federation was followed a little over a decade later by a similar division within the Bani Yas. The Al Bu Flasah tribe, headed by the Al Maktoum family, seceded from Abu Dhabi in 1833, to become independent in Dubai which had, until then, been part of Abu Dhabi's dominion.

The main thrust of the 1820 agreements with the area sheikhs was to keep the sea lanes free and clear for British vessels thus furthering British trade objectives in the Gulf. They wanted to limit competition as much as possible by restricting the abilities of the local tradesmen to conduct business and to lessen the likelihood of other foreign powers gaining a foothold in the region. They planned to dominate the area by forbidding anyone else to trade in the Gulf, using local ports and traders to supply goods to the northern part of Arabia, or even further north to the Mediterranean. For the most part they were successful in their efforts, virtually eliminating competition by using gunboat diplomacy to subdue the local coastal inhabitants who were, to all intents, incapable of defending themselves. In support of their position, the British established a Political Residency Agent in Sharjah in 1826 to report the affairs of the Trucial States to the British Political Resident in Bushire.

Despite their lack of choice in the matter, in some ways the people of the Trucial States hoped that the stronger presence of the British in the region would somehow improve their lives. Here was a powerful modern nation with many resources; surely some of their wealth - better arms perhaps, or finer ships - would somehow find its way into the hands of the local people. In a place where there was no local currency, where trade and barter were the main means of exchange, the British might have helped to establish a monetary system that could have strengthened the local economy thereby improving everyone's long term prospects, including their own. But none of that was to happen in the 1800s. The British would continue to dominate. Little of their wealth or their knowledge, however, was transferred to the region, leaving the inhabitants struggling with the same poverty and even fewer prospects for increased prosperity than they had previously.

In 1835 the British concluded a set of truce agreements between themselves and the sheikhs of the area. Almost twenty years later, the agreements, which had been renewed annually, became permanent.

The area then became known, to the British at least, as either the Trucial Coast or the Trucial States. The British wished to exercise control in the area thus securing peaceful passage for their trading vessels which were quite active along the Persian coast throughout the nineteenth century. Their trade flourished, particularly in the latter half of the century with the advent of telegraph lines as well as steamer and postal services.

At around the same time that the agreements became perpetual in 1853, events were occurring in India and on the other side of the Gulf which would influence the development of the Trucial States well into the next century.

Waves of migration from the Persian coast

Tired of the ever expanding influence of the British as well as their seemingly insatiable appetite for acquiring Indian lands, the people of some provinces of India revolted in 1857. The mutiny was suppressed by the British government who then abolished the East India Company and replaced it with a new administration under the British Crown in London. A Viceroy represented the crown in India and a secretary of state for India became a member of the British Cabinet. Although the insurgence meant the end of the powerful East India Company, the sub-continent would continue to be controlled by the British for another ninety years.

Meanwhile, on the Persian coast, change was imminent. Throughout the eighteenth and most of the nineteenth centuries the supply of Indian goods to the Trucial States depended mainly on the port of Linjah, where the British steam lines called regularly. Here, and at Sharjah, Dubai, Ras al Khaimah and Abu Dhabi, a few Indian traders (Banians), who were British subjects, began to settle. However, the commercial strength of the Persian coastal towns on the trade routes was to decline drastically when the government in Tehran began encroaching on the Arab tribes who had inhabited the area for generations. My own roots can be traced back to those who fled Persian oppression after the latter occupied the island of Sirri, near Abu Musa in the middle of the Persian Gulf, in 1887. By the end of the century the Persians would oust the Qawasim completely from Linjah, and the trading post which had once flourished would slide from prosperity to relative obscurity within the space of a few decades.

The Persian coastal area, which varies in width from five to fifty kilometres, is separated from the interior of the country by a range of mountains. For several centuries Shia Muslims had lived behind the mountains in the interior of the country while the coastal area overlooking the Gulf was inhabited mostly by Sunni Arabs. Because the Persian government wished to control the coast and the sea lanes, however, it began expanding its sphere of influence and building a naval force towards the middle of the nineteenth century. Encouraged by the Russians, who had allied themselves with the Shah, the Persians began moving from the central part of the country to the coastal area, where they took over the outlying Arabic-speaking villages and islands which were defenceless against such a threat. However, the Arabs and the Sunni Persians who lived and conducted their business on the coast were unwilling to submit to the will of the Persian Shia government in Tehran. They were either harassed or made to pay duties and taxes - some of the sheikhs of the islands were even imprisoned for failing to obey the government in Tehran so they began to leave the Persian coast from the 1870s onwards to settle on the other side of the Gulf in Dubai, Sharjah and Ras al Khaimah. As people moved from the Persian coast and the outlying islands to the Dubai side of the Gulf they brought with them their trade, their businesses, their shipping experience and their crafts skills. They also brought Indian citizens who were the links between the pearl divers and their markets around the world. The Indian merchants imported goods to supply the diving fleets and took pearls in payment for the supplies. These merchants collected pearls from all over the Gulf, took them to India for processing and then exported them to the European markets on the bigger ships that sailed from India. This drain of expertise was to be the foundation for Dubai's strong growth after 1902.

New agreements in 1892

Throughout the 1800s the British maintained an "arms-length" position on the internal affairs of the Trucial States as had been agreed in their treaties of both 1820 and 1853. Their interests lay primarily in protecting the sea lanes and their ability to trade freely with minimum competition; the internal affairs of the Trucial States were of little concern to them. They stood on the sidelines willing to let continuing tribal infighting and conflict between the various sheikhs and rulers occupy the rulers' time and energy. These squabbles served the British well. While local men and resources were tied up fighting each other the British were left to their own devices. Any alliance between the various tribes and sheikhs might have jeopardised the British position as the supreme power in the region; they were quite happy not to interfere with anything that allowed them to maintain their own privileged status. Other than the Political Agent in Sharjah, there was no British representative in the Trucial States so contact with the local rulers was minimal unless the British had some new demand of them in which case the Political

Resident from Bushire would come to convey Her Majesty's wishes. Towards the end of the century, however, the British felt it necessary, for several reasons, to conclude a new set of agreements with the ruling sheikhs.

The gradual development of British supremacy in the Gulf in the second half of the nineteenth century elicited an antagonistic reaction from the two dominant regional powers, Persia and the Ottomans. In May 1871 the Ottomans occupied Al Hasa and extended their influence to Qatar. When they claimed Bahrain and eight towns in the Trucial States as being part of the province of Nejd in 1872, Ottoman warships began to appear in the Gulf. In 1887 British authorities in the Gulf were also watchful of vigorous Persian activities in Qatar, Bahrain, Abu Dhabi and Dubai as well as their occupation of Sirri island. None of these developments unduly alarmed the British as they had a considerable presence and influence in the region. However, the situation changed in the late 1880s and early 1890s: the French, Russians and Germans entered the field for the first time. When two French arms dealers appeared in the Gulf in 1891 the British viewed their arrival as a potential threat to British supremacy in the area.

With some urgency, Major Talbot, the Political Resident in the Gulf at the time, visited the Trucial sheikhs seeking assurance that they would maintain their relationship with the British while rejecting any overtures from the newcomers. An exclusive treaty was signed by the various sheikhs during March 1892. The sheikhs agreed that neither they, their heirs, nor their successors, would, on any account, cede, sell, mortgage or otherwise give for occupation any part of their territory save to Her Majesty's Government. In return, the British pledged to protect the Trucial States against foreign aggression. This treaty, the main pillar of British authority in the Trucial States, became the model for later agreements signed with the sheikhs of Bahrain in the same year, Kuwait in 1899, and Qatar in 1935. The "treaty of protectorate" remained in force until the British withdrawal from the Gulf in 1971. To some degree the British were justified in their fears of the ruling sheikhs being susceptible to the advances of other foreign powers in the Gulf, particularly in the case of Sheikh Zayed bin Khalifa, who ruled Abu Dhabi between 1855 and 1909.

Sheikh Zayed bin Khalifa and the British

The Sheikhdom of Abu Dhabi, which had grown in size and strength in the nineteenth century, reached a peak under Zayed bin Khalifa, a gallant young warrior who assumed the rulership at the age of twenty. He had learnt the art of governing during a five year stay in

Dubai to which he had been exiled by the previous ruler. He was a skilled politician and diplomat who was quickly able to extend his authority from Abu Dhabi and the Liwa over the hinterland south of Al Ain to Ibri in the Dhahirah area.

During the first fifteen years of Sheikh Zayed bin Khalifa's fifty-four year rule, a series of events, including a single deadly fight with one of his contemporaries, contributed to his success in establishing himself as the dominant ruler in the area. He defeated Sheikh Khalid bin Sultan, ruler of Sharjah, in 1868, by killing him in one-on-one combat thus gaining much prestige and respect among the bedouin tribes. The hand-to-hand fight which resulted in the death of Sheikh Khalid changed the balance of power in the Trucial States, tipping it in favour of the Bani Yas tribes over the Qawasim.

During the 1870s and 1880s Sheikh Zayed bin Khalifa's authority in the interior gradually increased and Abu Dhabi became the strongest of the area's sheikhdoms with the largest pearling fleet. The richest of the pearl fisheries in the Gulf lay between the Qatar peninsula and Dubai; the island of Delma, in Abu Dhabi's waters, became the centre for provisioning the pearling fleets during the diving season. It was this bustling activity that eventually attracted my own grandfather, among others, to open up shop at Delma Island around the turn of the century.

At the height of his power, Sheikh Zayed bin Khalifa had plans to unify the Trucial States under his own rule, schemes which unfortunately never bore fruit due in part to his falling out with the local British authorities.

Several factors led to the rift between Sheikh Zayed and the British. First, in 1895, Sheikh Zayed expressed his intention to build a settlement on the island of Zora for his father-in-law Sheikh Nasir bin Salmin, head of the Sudan tribe. Zora, which lay between Ajman and Hamriyyah, had formerly been part of the Qawasim federation's territory. The Sheikh of Ajman protested to the British over the proposed settlement. They in turn pressured Zayed, under threat of bombardment, to abandon his plan.

Then, in 1896, Sheikh Zayed bin Khalifa encouraged the French by establishing commercial and political relations with them and offering Abu Dhabi as a port of call for their Messageries Maritimes. Two years later Sheikh Zayed's ally Seyyid Faisal bin Turki, the Sultan of Muscat, gave the French a coal depot at Jissah, south of Muscat, prompting the British to threaten the Sultan also with bombardment of his palace unless he revoked this concession to the French. In fear for his life and the safety of his people the Sultan complied.

The third and final straw came in 1905 when Sheikh Zayed, who had been entrusted with peacekeeping responsibilities in some territories belonging to the Sultan of Oman, had a disagreement with the Bani Qatab tribe who lived there. Sheikh Zayed imposed on them a large fine of around one hundred camels. When Sheikh Rashid bin Ahmed, ruler of Umm al Qaiwain, visited Zayed at his camp asking mercy on behalf of the Bani Qatab, Zayed took him prisoner and sent him to Abu Dhabi. In response, the British Political Resident, Major Cox, arrived in Abu Dhabi by ship, threatening to fire on the fort unless Sheikh Rashid was released. Sheikh Zayed finally produced Sheikh Rashid who was subsequently taken back to Umm al Qaiwain by Major Cox. In addition to putting an end to Sheikh Zayed's plans for unification, these incidents soured his relations with the British.

During the same period the British forced the sheikhs to give up the importation and purchase of arms and ammunition, completely disregarding the inhabitants' need to be armed for defensive purposes, as well as for pride and prestige. They tried to enforce a blockade of arms traffic in the Gulf between 1907 and 1913 during the late years of Sheikh Zayed bin Khalifa's rule. However, when they landed a force in Dubai to search for arms in 1910 they faced strong resistance and were forced to abandon the search almost immediately.

Although Sheikh Zayed bin Khalifa was not removed as ruler when he fell out of favour with the British, deposing a ruler was a strategy they sometimes used to ensure the loyalty of the sheikhs. When they sensed a ruler was not willing to cooperate or when they felt he was making too many demands, they worked behind the scenes using one pretext or another to replace him with a relative. They were successful in their efforts on several occasions, especially after the 1900s, first in Sharjah, then in Ras al Khaimah, then again in Sharjah. Those sheikhs who were vocal critics of the British, questioning their authority or defying their orders, were dealt with swiftly and effectively. All the while the British insisted their presence benefited the people of the area but in hindsight we know the benefits of their control were negligible.

Chapter 2

Unmet Expectations

Dawn of the twentieth century - troubled waters

At the turn of the century life in the Sheikhdom of Abu Dhabi was virtually the same as it had been a hundred years earlier. Not much progress had been made in the 1800s. In fact, if anything, the situation had deteriorated.

Shipping, trading and seafaring capabilities had been severely crippled in 1819 when the British destroyed first the Qawasim fleet, then most of the ships that lay at anchor along the Trucial States' coast. The shipbuilding industry was also wiped out, thus dramatically reducing the number of local vessels sailing in the Gulf for some time. The few which were built were smaller and capable of far shorter distances than their predecessors because of restrictions which had been imposed by the British as part of agreements signed after the bombardments. With trading possibilities severely curtailed the people were forced to rely even more on the meagre earnings derived from pearl diving.

Abu Dhabi was still a small settlement used primarily before the pearling season to prepare and supply the fleets for the summer's work. The people of the area were poor and the island village had little to offer so they sought better prospects inland, primarily in Al Ain and Liwa where there were some plantations and date trees. Even the ruler of the time, Sheikh Zayed bin Khalifa, resided mainly in Al Ain. Since pearl diving was still the only means of income it was difficult for the inhabitants to sustain the living standard enjoyed by many other Gulf sheikhdoms or towns of the time including Qatar (which was supported by the Saudis), Bahrain (where the British had fostered good relations since 1820) and Kuwait (which had flourished as a trading post during the days of the Ottoman empire). Abu Dhabians and their ruling sheikh, on the other hand, had no one to lean upon for support except those few, such as the Sultan of Oman, with whom they had friendly alliances or close relations.

Most of the northern sheikhdoms were in more or less the same position as Abu Dhabi - their economies were stagnant, living was simple, and the outlook for progress and growth in the near future was bleak. The exception was Dubai, which began to flourish after 1902.

The foundation for Dubai's growth in the early 1900s had been built over the previous three decades. From the 1870s onwards Sunni Arab businessmen and traders living on the Persian coast and nearby islands found it increasingly difficult to live under the ever-expanding control and influence of the Persian government in Tehran. Seeking better prospects and freedom from domination they emigrated to Dubai in several waves throughout the latter part of the nineteenth century. Persia's loss was Dubai's gain.

These immigrants had been trading with India for a long time and had forged strong business relationships with merchants on the sub-continent. When they settled in Dubai they brought with them their knowledge, their ambition and their contacts. So it was that in 1902 a steam-powered vessel bypassed the Persian coastal city of Linjah, until then the main trading post for all incoming ships from India, to unload its goods in Dubai instead. In so doing the first direct sea lane between India and Dubai was established, circumventing Linjah which had been one of the steam line's most important ports of call in the Gulf for nearly forty years. In this way, the traders avoided the newly imposed Persian tariffs and customs duties. Without the regular steamer visits, the city of Linjah, a bustling trading centre, quickly declined.

The standard of living in Dubai, on the other hand, improved. More ships stopped there to unload their goods, some of which were destined for Dubai itself, some of which were transported overland to the interior of Oman, Abu Dhabi and the rest of the Trucial States. Trade growth has been claimed as a benefit of the British presence in the Gulf. However, it was Arab, Indian and Persian traders who were responsible for establishing the trade and communication links between Dubai and India from the 1900s onwards.

As Dubai jumped ahead in leaps and bounds, two major factors held Abu Dhabi back during the early years of the twentieth century, inhibiting the sheikhdom's prospects for growth. The first was the internal power struggle between members of the ruling family; the second was the first world war.

Abu Dhabi had been ruled, relatively peacefully and uneventfully, for over fifty years by Sheikh Zayed bin Khalifa. When he died in 1909 he was succeeded by his son Sheikh Tahnoun who ruled for only three years before he also died. He was in turn succeeded by his brother Hamdan bin Zayed who ruled until 1922 when he was assassinated by his brother Sheikh Sultan – the father of the present ruler Sheikh Zayed bin Sultan – after a decade of conflict and disagreement. Only five years later, in 1927, Sheikh Sultan was himself assassinated by another brother Saqr who was in turn assassinated the following year by another brother's bodyguard.

This decade-long family strife, rooted for the most part in greed, was aided and abetted by British practices and policies at the time. When a British ship arrived in the Gulf, for example, the ruler would often visit it in a small boat and subsequently be seen bringing back a despatch box given to him by the Political Resident. Members of his family assumed wrongly that this box contained money and presents whereas it probably held only papers. The family thought the ruler was hoarding money for himself which they felt should be shared. According to oral history, however, when a safe belonging to one of the assassinated rulers was forced open after his death it contained a single rupee, a clear indication that the jealous members of the ruling family were sadly mistaken in their assumptions. The British never paid any money or gave anything to the rulers – it may have looked as if they showered them with gifts of cash and in kind but this was not the case. Nevertheless, if family members suspected a ruler of deceit they frequently turned against him causing infighting which sometimes resulted in death, or deaths, as it did in the 1920s.

Although the British may not have been actively involved in the murder and intrigue that went on during this period, as it was their policy not to interfere in internal politics, they certainly used intra-tribal or intra-familial conflict to their advantage when it suited their purposes. If a ruler did not support them they became willing partners in ploys that might lead to him being deposed and replaced with another sheikh who was more receptive to their demands. Every sheikh who took over as ruler began with lots of ambition and goodwill towards the British but as time passed each was disappointed and the relationship would soon deteriorate. On the other hand, when the British realised the sheikh was no longer their puppet, they either devised a means to remove him and replace him with a relative, or they contrived to ignore him completely. Such was the case with both Sheikh Zayed bin Khalifa who was ignored by the British for the last decade of his fifty-nine-year rule which had begun in 1850 and the Ruler of Ras al Khaimah who was deposed in 1948.

Regardless of the causes, the internal strife, ongoing feuding and frequent changes in leadership between members of the ruling family during the first part of the twentieth century left Abu Dhabi floating aimlessly like a rudderless ship in stormy seas. Abu Dhabi did not become peaceful or stabilise again until 1928 when Sheikh Shakhbut bin Sultan, one of the sons of the assassinated ruler Sultan bin Zayed, took over. Because of the constant turmoil and instability in Abu Dhabi between 1909 and 1928 there was little development. In addition, progress was inhibited by the larger international conflict which had flared concurrently.

During the first world war there were fewer large ships in service between Bahrain and Abu Dhabi thus virtually cutting off the much needed dates which fed the people in Abu Dhabi. They became even more dependent on what was grown in the oases of Liwa, Al Ain or the northern territories. The demand often exceeded the supply resulting in food shortages and hunger. In addition to slowing worldwide trade, the war also reduced the demand for pearls which in turn badly affected the Gulf pearl industry. It was a very difficult period for the people in the Trucial States.

The Shakhbut years

There was renewed hope when Sheikh Shakhbut took over in 1928. As the new ruler, he was confident that the British would support him financially thus enabling him to carry his people into the new century. The people were optimistic too and prayed that Sheikh Shakhbut would change their fortunes, bringing them opportunities for prosperity and modernisation. Sheikh Shakhbut was young - only twenty four when he became ruler - and people believed his youth and energy would help open the doors to the future. The first world war was now a decade behind them, peace was established and trade was resuming between the western nations. The pearl industry had recovered somewhat from the downturn it had experienced during the war years and an enthusiastic new leader stood at the helm. At last Abu Dhabians looked forward with anticipation to a brighter tomorrow. There was an optimistic expectation that the hard days were over and a new day was dawning. Sadly this was not to be the case.

Like his predecessors, Sheikh Shakhbut found to his dismay that the British were not prepared to assist him financially. Almost every ruling sheikh had fallen into the trap of expecting the British to assist them to help their people; Shakhbut was no exception. But he too quickly learned that his expectations were unfounded; the British contributed nothing whatsoever to the development of Abu Dhabi. The thirty-eight years of Shakhbut's rule, which ended in 1966, were characterised by general stagnation of the economy in Abu Dhabi, intermittent declines caused by various other factors including the second world war, threats to the sheikhdom's borders and continuing disputes with the British.

The twenty to thirty years preceding the beginning of Shakbut's rule had been turbulent. At the same time, however, there was a fairly strong and sustained demand for pearls which was interrupted only during the first world war. Unfortunately, the only people who really benefited from pearling were the merchants, most of whom were Indians. They bought the pearls and re-sold them in India to wholesalers who then distributed them to the rest of the world. India was the centre for gathering all the pearls produced from the Gulf. Whether they were from the Trucial States' coast, Bahrain or Kuwait, they were all sent there before being transformed into jewellery and re-exported to the West or the Far East. Had the pearl buyers - the French, the German, the Swiss and even the Spanish and Portuguese - been able to come to the area and buy directly from the source, the demand for pearls, as well as the prices, might have been better. But they were forbidden by the British. So it was the Indians instead (themselves British subjects), who channelled everything to Bombay thus enjoying a virtual monopoly on the region's pearl industry. One notable exception to the ban on foreign buyers was Cartier, the French designer, who came to Bahrain in the 1930s and 1940s to purchase pearls. How he managed the visits is a mystery - he must have been either accompanied by a British businessman, citizen, or diplomat, or given special permission. By that time, however, the industry had already seen the last of its better days.

The beginning of the end of the mean existence that typified pearling in the Gulf came in the 1930s, only a few short years after Sheikh Shakhbut came to power. Following the first world war, the Japanese began cultivating cultured pearls, which, once the practice and the pearls were accepted on world markets, resulted in a huge drop in the price of natural pearls. This led to an almost immediate and virtually complete collapse of the pearling industry in the Gulf, leaving some of the local pearl merchants who were unable to sell their pearls in dire financial straits.

The pearl industry in the Gulf depended on a system of capital financing which proved the undoing of several local traders when the market for natural pearls bottomed out. Each year the local traders either borrowed money or were advanced supplies, mostly from Banian lenders and merchants residing in the Trucial States, to finance the yearly pearling expeditions. After the season, the capital, and substantial interest, would be repaid once the traders had returned from India where they sold the year's take, or the traders would settle their debts with the merchants with the pearls themselves. When the market for natural pearls collapsed some of the traders were unable to sell their pearls or were forced to sell them at a loss, thus making it impossible to repay their loans. The Banian money lenders, who, although they resided in the Trucial States, were Indians and thus British subjects, complained to the British authorities in the area that the locals were defaulting on their loans. As British subjects the Banians were under the protection of British naval ships that patrolled the area. When disagreements occurred over non-payment of debts the British political agent pressured the ruling sheikh to pay up on behalf of the debtor or risk bombardment of his town. Unfortunately this happened on several occasions between 1930 and 1945 in Abu Dhabi. These incidents would be the first in a long series of disagreements which poisoned the relationship between the British and Sheikh Shakhbut.

Nevertheless, the failure of the pearl industry, devastating though it was initially to the local traders and the populace as a whole, proved to be a blessing in disguise as the years went by. True, it had been the inhabitants' only means of survival, but the end of pearling liberated them from the annual torment they had endured for centuries. Unfortunately the inhabitants of Abu Dhabi waited a good twenty years before the promise of oil reserves in the region opened up new employment opportunities for them. By then the chance to earn a living doing almost anything was welcomed by one and all.

The race is on

With the extraction and subsequent exportation of oil from Bahrain in 1932, interest in the region's oil resources intensified throughout the 1930s, 40s and 50s. Having signed, then re-affirmed, agreements that prohibited the rulers and sheikhs from communicating with any other nation, the British had a significant advantage in the race to exploit our oil resources. In 1935 the Trucial States sheikhs, including Shakhbut, signed oil exploration options for their respective territories. With the income generated as a result, the Ruler decided to build Abu Dhabi's first palace – a large labour intensive project that lasted for about four years. The palace project mobilised most of Abu Dhabi's available vessels to import building materials such as rocks and clay from across the Gulf. In addition, almost all the able-bodied men of the sheikhdom were employed either directly or indirectly on its construction. This generated income for the inhabitants of Abu Dhabi from 1936 to 1939 when the project was completed. Using the only boat they had at the time, my father and uncles participated in the project by transporting rock, which was used in the palace walls, from the island of Ras Ghurab, a day's sail from Abu Dhabi Island. Although it made use of our resources and injected some money into the local economy the palace was the only such project undertaken at the time. It was not enough to sustain people now that the pearl industry was dead.

As the palace was being built in Abu Dhabi the British-owned oil companies began inducing the ruling sheikhs to sign concession agreements giving them exclusive rights to the oil that lay beneath the desert and the sea beds. The first of the Trucial States rulers to grant such a concession was the Ruler of Dubai who signed an agreement in May 1937. The Ruler of Sharjah followed suit in December and the Rulers of Ras al Khaimah and Kalba were both on board by December 1938.

Sheikh Shakhbut, however, demurred. Knowing the terms of the Americans' agreement with the Saudis as well as the Bahrain Petroleum Company (BAPCO) agreement with the Bahrainis, he held out a little longer for better terms and conditions. In the end, however, he too signed a concession agreement in 1939. He was paid 300,000 rupees for signing the concession; it was to be followed by additional income during the exploration and production phases. Unfortunately, a few months later the second world war began.

As the war raged on it led to a period of depression in Abu Dhabi. Despite the fact that a concession agreement had been signed nothing further was done about developing the oil sector as the British were preoccupied with the war effort. The demand for Gulf pearls was now virtually non-existent, trade was sluggish, food was even scarcer than it had been before and most Abu Dhabians had few employment prospects. As a result many people emigrated from Abu Dhabi to other parts of either the sheikhdom (Al Ain and the Liwa), the Trucial States (Dubai primarily) or the Gulf generally (Doha, Bahrain, Qatar and Kuwait).

Border disputes

Six months after the second world war ended the ruler of Dubai threatened to take part of Abu Dhabi's territory. He transported some of his men by sea to a place called Ghanada, near where the Al Jazira resort stands today, and laid claim to the territory between there and the Abu Dhabi - Dubai border. Sheikh Shakhbut was forced to mobilise his own men in defence while he attempted to defuse the situation using diplomatic channels. He felt victimised by both the ruler of Dubai, who posed the direct threat, and the British whom he had hoped would assist him financially if not militarily in his fight against the unprovoked aggression. Naturally the British tried to distance themselves as they had signed treaties with all the Trucial States' sheikhs and tended to avoid getting involved in internal squabbles unless it was to their benefit to do so. Nevertheless Shakhbut persisted in his political and diplomatic efforts and, after much manoeuvreing, he finally managed to corner the British into taking his side against the ruler of Dubai. In the 1892 agreements signed by the Trucial States' rulers there was a clause prohibiting the transportation of troops by sea. The clause further stated that a ruler or sheikh who contravened the prohibition would be considered the aggressor in any ensuing conflict. Of course the clause had been intended to protect the British sea lanes and trading interests in the Gulf at the end of the previous century. However, Sheikh Shakhbut used the old treaty to his advantage and forced the British into an awkward position. They were unable to ignore their contractual agreement of 1892 and found themselves obligated to put pressure on the aggressor to withdraw from Ghanada. The ruler of Dubai was subsequently fined 200,000 rupees for violating the rules of the fifty-four year old treaty.

As soon as the situation at Ghanada was settled, things began to come to a head at the Buraimi oasis which the Saudis had tried to claim, off and on, for nearly a century and a half. The history of the dispute stretched back to the beginning of the nineteenth century. At that time the villages of the Buraimi region were divided between the Naim, Al Bu Shamis and the Dhawahir tribes. The villages of Buraimi, Sara and Hamasa were inhabited mainly by the Naim and Al Bu Shamis who were loyal to the Sultan of Oman. The Al Dhawahir tribes who inhabited Muwayje, Mutarid, Qattarah, Miraijib, Jimi, Hili and Al Ain were loyal to the Ruler of Abu Dhabi. When the first Saudi expedition reached Buraimi in 1800, it faced strong resistance from the combined forces of Sheikh Shakhbut bin Dyab, the Ruler of Abu Dhabi from 1793 to 1816, and the Sultan of Muscat. The resistance was not enough, however, to keep the Naim and Al Bu Shamis from adopting the Saudis' Wahhabi doctrine during the Saudi presence in the oasis. After the fall of the Saudi capital in Dariyyah, south of Riyadh, in 1818, the Saudis were forced to forfeit their claim on Buraimi thereby relinquishing it once again to the Sultan of Muscat. At the same time, the new Ruler of Abu Dhabi, Tahnoun bin Shakhbut, re-established his authority in Al Ain and its environs.

When the Saudis returned to power in 1843, they again sent a representative to Buraimi. Five years later Sheikh Said bin Tahnoun, who ruled Abu Dhabi from 1845 to 1855, defeated the Saudis at Al Anka which lies between Abu Dhabi and Al Ain. Finally, Sheikh Zayed bin Khalifa, who ruled after Said bin Tahnoun, cooperated with the Sultan of Oman to expel the Saudi forces from Buraimi in 1869.

The dispute flared again more than sixty years later when King Abdul Aziz signed an oil concession with the American oil company SOCAL in 1933 and claimed part of Abu Dhabi's lands in the west as well as the Buraimi oasis as part of his ancestral domain. Negotiations to settle the frontiers went on for four years but the situation remained unresolved. A decade later, a group of American geologists accompanied by some armed Saudi guards, camped near Sila in the western part of Abu Dhabi. The British Political Officer from Sharjah, accompanied by Sheikh Zayed's brother Sheikh Hazza, visited their camp insisting they withdraw from the area. The group left but the incident sparked a new round of disagreements.

As a result, the British felt it necessary to take steps to defend the rights of their oil companies. In an effort to impose order in the desert and protect their oil exploration teams, they formed a small military force called the Trucial Oman Scouts. Based in Sharjah, the force consisted of about 200 local soldiers commanded by a handful of British officers. Their mandate was to patrol the area and keep the peace.

The border conflicts intensified throughout the 1950s. In 1952 Turki bin Utaishan, a Saudi representative, arrived in Buraimi accompanied by forty men in civilian dress. He set himself up in the village of Hamasa, raised the Saudi flag and began distributing money and gifts amongst the people. He then invited the local inhabitants to his camp where he provided hearty meals for all visitors. His tactics were hard to resist at a time when most of the region's people were poor and hungry. Meanwhile, the Saudis also supported their claim with gifts of gold to the local tribal chiefs.

In 1954 Ibn Nami replaced Turki bin Utaishan. A year later the Saudis and the British agreed to refer the border dispute to an international tribunal which, like the efforts before it, failed to resolve the issue. In October 1955 the Sultan of Oman and the Ruler of Abu Dhabi, supported by the Trucial Oman Scouts, moved into the Buraimi Oasis and raided Ibn Nami's house in Hamasa. Although the British had a degree of self-interest in the outcome of this dispute there is no doubt that without their support and intervention Abu Dhabi and Oman would have lost much of their territory to Saudi Arabia. The Buraimi dispute was finally settled peacefully in 1975 when an agreement was signed between Saudi Arabia, Abu Dhabi and Oman.

Two other border disputes worsened Sheikh Shakbut's already poor relationship with the British. In 1952, in Dammam, a conference was held to try to resolve some of the ongoing border problems. At that conference Sheikh Shakhbut claimed that Abu Dhabi's western frontier extended to Umm Said on the coast of the peninsula also claimed by Qatar. In the end, the conference settled nothing. Later on, in 1958, Qatar granted an oil concession to the Shell Oil Company on the island of Halul which had always been claimed by Sheikh Shakhbut and recognised by the British as belonging to Abu Dhabi. When a special court was convened by the British in 1961 to rule on the Halul affair Sheikh Shakhbut refused to appear, nor would he submit any documentation to support his cause. The court decided in favour of the Qatari claim. Sheikh Shakhbut blamed the British for both the Umm Said and Halul incidents, neither of which was resolved to his satisfaction.

Despite the disputes, prospects for the sheikhdom looked much brighter in the 1950s. Throughout the second half of the decade all signs pointed toward the imminent discovery of oil in Abu Dhabi territory. Exploration, both on land and offshore, was gathering momentum and more local people were being employed in exploration, development and drilling. Granted they were mostly labourers, but at least they were employed. With the possibility of striking oil so close to becoming a reality, hope and anticipation of a better life were at an all-time high throughout the sheikhdom. When a promising show of oil was discovered at Murban in December 1959 the people of Abu Dhabi heaved a collective sigh of relief – hard times were over, they were on the verge of prosperity and wealth. Or so they thought at the time. Unfortunately it would be another seven years, under the rulership of Sheikh Zayed, before the discovery began to have any beneficial effect on the daily lives of the local people.

Meanwhile the British pressured Sheikh Shakhbut to contribute part of his oil revenues to finance the development in surrounding sheikhdoms. They wanted a commitment from him to pay for the expenses of other Trucial States which did not have as much oil. He, on the other hand, believed that the British should be playing a more active role in supporting the other sheikhs to whom he felt he owed nothing. He saw no reason to stand as guarantor for their expenditure, particularly since one of them had tried to invade his territory a mere six years previously. The pressure on him mounted, however.

After three decades of rule, all of which were rife with conflict with the British, Sheikh Shakhbut had become mistrustful, wary and cautious. Having learned through experience that they would not support him financially he saved all he could in anticipation of such situations recurring in the future. Royalties from the oil concession had been paid yearly for almost a decade by the time oil was actually discovered in commercial quantities. But instead of being used to develop the sheikhdom, the monies were accumulating in the custody of Sheikh Shakhbut who was unwilling to part with a penny in case he should need the money to mobilise forces in response to some external threat. He became increasingly stubborn in his negotiations with the oil companies, forcing them to advance him money in ever greater amounts. He mistrusted the British and feared being left vulnerable if he spent the proceeds so he continued to stockpile the funds for an emergency. Nevertheless, he finally agreed, under duress, that when oil was found in his territory he would spend four per cent of the resulting revenues towards the development of the other sheikhdoms.

High hopes

While the coffers filled with oil revenues, some of which were financing development in the other Trucial States, Abu Dhabi remained the most backward and primitive of all the sheikhdoms. In 1960 the inhabitants still lived from hand to mouth. Incomes were far below the poverty line; many people went hungry and some even resorted to hunting dhubs to feed themselves and their families. There were no medical facilities to treat the sick and the first non-religious school, ill-equipped as it was, had opened only the previous year. Nevertheless, we saw signs with our own eyes that indicated we should be moving forward. We witnessed an increase in the number of foreigners in Abu Dhabi as well as an upsurge in the movement of oil-related equipment and heavy trucks. New companies set up camps in the desert and on Das Island and hired locals to work for them as drivers, watchmen and labourers. We all knew oil had been discovered. There was a general atmosphere of expectation. Yet there was no confirmation of the discovery from the Ruler's office or even from the Ruler himself. Privately, Abu Dhabians had many questions: Was the discovery significant? What would it mean for us? How would our lives be changed? Who would manage the development that would surely be taking place soon? When would we have hospitals and schools? Publicly, however, no one said a word. Most of the time it seemed the foreigners knew more about what was going on in Abu Dhabi than the inhabitants themselves. Abu Dhabians thought that perhaps the Ruler's palace was unsure of the quantity of oil, the viability of the reserves or the potential revenues, and while these were being confirmed there would be no official news. It was confusing to everyone but the local people were so grateful for the opportunity to work and thus improve their lot that none voiced their concerns.

The days, weeks and months went by without any significant change. No new departments or government institutions were set up to manage the oil or the oil revenues, no hospitals or schools were established, nothing was done to improve the lives of the people who lived here. People became somewhat resigned to the fact that we seemed stuck in the nineteenth century. They began to accept the status quo. As a result, when massive change finally did begin some years later, none of the people here were ready for it. We would be caught unprepared, ill-equipped, poorly-educated and overwhelmed by the intensity of the tidal wave of change that would eventually transform our lives forever.

Chapter 3

Generations in the Gulf

A short family history

My family has always lived in the Gulf region; I have traced our history back several generations. My great-grandfather was the independent ruler of an Arab village called Harmoud located in the mountains on the southern coast of Persia, the country known since the 1930s as Iran. He governed the village during the early part of the 1800s, just as his father and grandfather before him had done. Each in his turn took care of the people of the village, most of whom were engaged primarily in agriculture rather than fishing because they were located quite far from the sea. Harmoud was also on a well-travelled trade route used by the caravans coming from the coastal settlements of Bandar-Abbas and Linjah, both of which were flourishing trading ports throughout the seventeenth, eighteenth and nineteenth centuries. So the people of the town governed by my forefathers were active in the transit and trading businesses as well as agricultural pursuits.

When my great-grandfather died in the 1880s, his eldest son, my great-uncle, replaced him as ruler of Harmoud. But my grandfather – the youngest son who had not yet reached his teens at the time of my great-grandfather's death – spurned a political life for one which allowed him to pursue his interest in books and literature.

Towards the middle of the nineteenth century the central government of Persia gradually began expanding its control from Tehran and extending its reach to include most of the outlying villages and towns near the Gulf coast. Encouraged by the Russians, the Persians began moving from the interior of the country and impinging on territories belonging to Arabs who had lived there for hundreds of years. My ancestors, having managed their own affairs independently of any central government for generations, did not take well to this expansionist movement of the central authority in Tehran. Like other Arab tribes in their area and the Qawasim in Linjah, they rebelled, fighting hard against the intruding Persians who unfortunately had a far bigger and better-equipped military machine which soon quashed any resistance that sprang up in the outlying towns and villages. Like many of the other coastal inhabitants my ancestors were at first unwilling to comply with the directives of the Persians. But they were unable to continue their resistance against the strong military presence in the area for any length of time and eventually were forced to submit to the will of Tehran, obeying its rules and regulations whether they agreed with them or not. The Arab governors and rulers of these towns and villages became the unwilling citizens of the Persian government that dictated their lives from far away.

Like many of his Arab compatriots, my grandfather, who was still very young and not particularly interested in politics or power, decided to emigrate from the Arab-dominated area of the Persian coast. In the mid 1880s, at about the age of fifteen, he crossed the Gulf to settle in Dubai. Once there, he stayed with relatives and continued his education through the mullas in Sharjah. A few years later he had the opportunity to get involved in a trading venture and before long he had opened a shop in the souk with a relative of his, Ibrahim Rais. Their venture was a resounding success. They prospered by trading with the shipping fleets that criss-crossed the Gulf between Dubai and their former homeland on the Persian coast. Unfortunately just before the turn of the century, the Dubai souk, which was, like most structures at the time, built of palm fronds, burned down in a terrible fire. All the shops, including that of my grandfather and his relative, were destroyed.

During the same era Abu Dhabi and Delma Islands were becoming important service centres for the pearl diving industry. Seeing potential there, my grandfather moved from Dubai around the beginning of century and settled in Abu Dhabi. In about 1905 he married a woman from the Al Hawamil tribe, one of the Bani Yas tribes of Abu Dhabi. His marriage was attended by the Ruler of Abu Dhabi, Sheikh Zayed Bin Khalifa, as a gesture of respect and a sign of my grandfather's standing in the community of Abu Dhabi. He was blessed with four sons and three daughters in addition to business success. He was soon considered one of the prominent citizens of Abu Dhabi: an important merchant and a man who commanded respect, partly because he came from a long line of governors called "kalountar" (or chief in Farsi), a name by which he was always called. When in Abu Dhabi he was a welcome member in the majlis of the rulers, at first Sheikh Tahnoun, then his brother Hamdan, then Sultan, and after him Saqr. Considered a wise and capable advisor, one of a few learned men in Abu Dhabi who had studied both literature and history and who could read and write, my grandfather was frequently sought out for his advice and counsel. Before long he had built up a new business and owned a number of boats, some of which he hired out during the pearl diving season and others which he himself captained. The demand for pearls was at a peak before the first world war and my grandfather's boating business, along with a small shop he opened in Abu Dhabi, flourished for a number of years until he suffered another misfortune in 1910.

His shop was one of a dozen or so leased out to local merchants by the landlord who owned the Abu Dhabi souk. In an act of vengeance after a disagreement with her husband, the wife of the landlord set fire to the souk. Just as had happened in Dubai, all the shops and the goods contained there were destroyed. My grandfather lost his second shop and his business was dealt a crippling blow. Mercifully the shipping side of his enterprise remained intact. He took stock of his affairs and decided to move his operation from Abu Dhabi to Delma Island where he established yet another shop. The island was the focus of much trading activity associated with the pearl diving industry. There was a large market from which the pearl divers got their supplies, food and water. My grandfather had boats as well as a shop so he was perfectly positioned to take advantage of the opportunities offered at Delma over the next six or seven years. During that time he travelled extensively, spending the summers on Delma and wintering with the family on Abu Dhabi island.

His business on Delma Island continued to thrive well into the 1920s despite a slump in the pearl industry during the first world war. My grandfather brought his elder sons, who were in their teens at the time, to the island to help him and be trained in the family business. They all continued to travel back and forth between the two islands, Abu Dhabi and Delma, spending half the year in each place. In fact most of the local men spent the summer months on Delma Island when the pearl season was in full swing, while the women and younger children lived in Al Ain. Then, during the winter they would all gather and live together with their respective families in Abu Dhabi.

Sadly, in 1928, my grandfather suffered a third stroke of bad luck. He was hosting some visitors in his Delma Island house which was adjacent to his shop there. The cook woke up early in the morning, lit the fire to make breakfast then left to gather wood outside. A breeze came up, fanning the sparks onto the palm fronds of which the kitchen walls were made. Soon the walls, then the whole house, were ablaze. In the blink of an eye the fire spread throughout the settlement at Delma destroying all the shops and most of the houses in its path before spreading to some of the boats which lay anchored off the beach. So devastating was the fire's destruction that the once thriving town never recovered. It declined, in a very short time, from an active trading post and pearl diving centre to a small settlement inhabited almost exclusively by fishermen.

My grandfather, my father and my uncles returned to Abu Dhabi, their fleet of six boats having been reduced by the fire to a single vessel. After this third fire my grandfather was reluctant to start his business anew so he settled back to a more religious life in Abu Dhabi leaving it up to his four sons, including my father, to pick up the pieces of the shipping business using the one remaining boat left undamaged. It was a difficult time as they tried to rebuild their lives having lost almost everything they possessed, but they were young and fit and were quite successful in whatever they tried.

Over the next ten or fifteen years they used the boat for fishing and shipping, transporting and trading goods across the Gulf between the ports of Abu Dhabi, Dubai and Linjah on the Persian coast, sometimes even sailing as far as Bahrain to trade. During the summers they still dived for pearls even though the returns from pearling worsened with each passing year. However, my father and uncles were all good divers so they were still in high demand by the captains who needed the strongest and healthiest men to continue working for them.

In the meantime foreign oil companies were taking a greater interest in the possibility of exploring for oil in Abu Dhabi, particularly since oil had already been found throughout the Gulf region. When Sheikh Shakhbut signed an oil option in 1935, he decided to build Abu Dhabi's first palace, which is now known as the "old fort", with the proceeds. The palace project, which started in 1936 and took about four years to complete, mobilised the entire workforce and most of the sea-going vessels available in Abu Dhabi at the time. The project, the only one of its kind in those days, was a godsend as the pearl diving industry had fallen off drastically after 1930 and the inhabitants had few prospects for earning a living. Using their only boat, which they manned themselves, my father and uncles participated in the project by transporting rocks from the island of Ras Ghurab to Abu Dhabi, about a two-day round trip. The palace still stands today in the heart of the city centre - a reminder of Abu Dhabi's first tentative steps toward the future and a testament to the quality of the building materials and workmanship, primitive though they were by today's standards, that were used in its construction.

It was on one of these rock hauling expeditions, in the late 1930s, that my father's friendship with Sheikh Zayed bin Sultan began. Sheikh Zayed, who was travelling between Abu Dhabi and Al Ain, had decided to journey part of the way by boat - it was a shorter route which also allowed him to leave his camels in the desert where there was better grazing than on the island of Abu Dhabi. On his return trip to Al Ain the caravan awaited Sheikh Zayed on the mainland near Ras Ghurab, the island from which my father and uncles were transporting the rock, so it was convenient for him to travel with them on their boat. During the trip - which entailed both sailing the vessel when there was wind as well as rowing it when there was none - Sheikh Zayed became better acquainted with my father and was much impressed with his skills as a man of letters. My father was one of the few people at the time who could read and write and Sheikh Zayed needed someone who was proficient in those skills, so he asked my father to join him and his family near Al Ain where he resided at the time. When Sheikh Zayed left the boat to rendezvous with his men and the caravan he did so with a promise from my father that he would give the proposal serious consideration. It was only a few months before my father decided to move to the Al Ain area where he soon became one of Sheikh Zayed's closest advisors and friends. Their brotherly relationship, which started on the sea in the mid-thirties, continues to this day.

Simple lives

In 1946, several years after he went to Muwayje, the village near Al Ain where Sheikh Zayed lived, my father married my mother. My elder sister was born in 1947, and I, their first son, arrived the following year. Life in the Sheikhdom of Abu Dhabi at the time of my birth was the same as it had been in 1800 - primitive. It remained that way throughout the years of my youth.

In 1950 the population of the sheikhdom, which included Al Ain and the Liwa oasis, was still very sparse. On the island of Abu Dhabi itself it had reached a peak of nearly 6,000 souls at the beginning of the century but by the mid-1950s had declined to about one-third of that because of the collapse of the pearl industry and the subsequent emigration of many inhabitants to Al Ain, the Liwa and other parts of the Gulf. The people who lived here were of several different tribes including the Manasir, Mazarea, Abu Mehair, Hawamil, Besadr, and Mehairi all of which fell under the umbrella of the Bani Yas. On the island of Abu Dhabi itself the tribes intermingled more than they did in the desert where there was space for them to spread out and establish territories each of which was controlled by a single tribe. In the desert the tribes kept to their own encampments which were often separated from those of other tribes by several days travel by camel.

The harsh weather conditions on the coast made people reluctant to live on Abu Dhabi island, especially in the extreme summer heat and high humidity. Women and children - including my mother, my aunts, myself and my siblings - moved either to Al Ain or the Liwa while the men were out pearl diving from May until September. Hardly anyone - five per cent of the total population at most - stayed in Abu Dhabi year-round because of the lack of fresh water and the poor living conditions. People only began staying throughout the year from the late 1960s onwards when businesses and offices were permanently established here.

Of course any long-distance trips were made on the back of a camel. There were very few mechanised vehicles, and no roads upon which to drive them anyway, so camels were still used extensively to travel between the towns and villages in the area. The northern sheikhdoms such as Dubai, Sharjah and Ras al Khaimah were reached primarily by boat. It still took about seven days to travel between Abu Dhabi and Al Ain or the Liwa and three or four days to Dubai. People usually travelled in a caravan of twenty or thirty camels for security and companionship. Until the late 1950s none of the local Abu Dhabians owned a car with the exception of the sheikh, a few members of the ruling family and the odd individual who had a vehicle which was used for taxi or transportation services. So the majority continued to rely on camels. About a decade before the arrival of the first vehicles my family suffered a great tragedy during a caravan trip.

During the 1940s and 1950s, and even as late as the 1960s, my family spent the winter months in Abu Dhabi and the summers in Al Ain, travelling back and forth by camel caravan in the spring and the autumn. In the autumn of 1947, about a year before my birth, my grandfather, grandmother and the women of the family joined a caravan headed from Al Ain to Abu Dhabi. A day into the trip they had camped for the night in an area called Sulaymat, near where the Al Ain airport is located today. Sometime in the evening my grandmother, who was about fifty-five, complained of feeling ill, so they laid her down on the ground to rest. In a few hours she was dead. Of course it was a terrible shock to the whole family: my grandmother had been strong and in good health and her death was completely unexpected. As is required in Islam they buried her there before the end of the next day and continued on toward Abu Dhabi.

Three days later, in a place called Remah near where Al Hasna is now, my grandfather fell ill and he too died suddenly. There were no other men from our family on the trip - they were in Abu Dhabi awaiting the return of my grandfather, the women and the children. So the other men in the caravan - the hired camel drivers and other travellers - got together and performed the burial ritual for my grandfather. Of course it was not uncommon for people, particularly the elderly, to die making trips across the desert. The causes of such deaths were usually sun stroke or travel fatigue resulting from the inescapable rays of the sun, which were scorching hot, and the constant motion of the camels which the travellers rode for days on end. It was too much to bear for the older people who no longer had the strength and endurance of their youth. Still, the deaths of both parents within a few days of each other on one trip dealt a cruel blow to my aunts. They were completely crushed with grief.

Nevertheless the caravan moved on and arrived in Abu Dhabi three days later with all the women in mourning. Of course my father and uncles were equally devastated when they heard the tragic news. In their sadness and grief the whole family could do nothing but accept the passing of my grandparents as the will of God. They carried on with their lives living simply and humbly like their friends and neighbours.

At that time both the permanent and seasonal residents of Abu Dhabi island still lived in barasti huts built of palm fronds harvested from the date trees. The exceptions were a few wealthier residents and the ruling family who lived in earth or clay houses; of course the ruling sheikh stayed in the palace. The houses were clustered together for security, companionship and warmth during the cooler months. People tried to build away from the sea if possible. Those further away from the water were more sheltered from the cold winter winds and the high humidity in spring, summer and autumn. We normally used mats woven from palm fronds as flooring in the tents and huts. During winter they were also fastened around the perimeter of the shelter to keep the cold shamal winds out and the warmth in. We made do with very little, using the same things for a variety of purposes. The woven palm mats, for example, were used for sitting, sleeping and insulating the tent. Sometimes they were even fashioned into roofs for the huts. We had no more clothes in winter than we had in summer so when it was cold the whole family huddled in one corner of the hut to keep warm at night. In the summer we slept outside in the open air where there was at least the possibility of being refreshed by a soft breeze. Wind towers were used to cool the houses which were built of mud or clay but most people had to suffer the excruciating heat of spring, summer and autumn with no hope of relief. Some nights the humidity was so high I felt as if I were sleeping rolled up in a wet blanket, sure that I could hear the lapping sound of water every time I turned over on my mat.

A daily struggle

During the winter months in Abu Dhabi town the women took care of the household including cooking, cleaning and caring for the children while the men fished. The women sold the catch at the market where they could then purchase household items, dry goods and food with the proceeds. They were also responsible for fetching water. They carried it from the wells either in goatskin bags slung down their backs from leather headbands across their foreheads or in clay urns balanced on their heads. The communal wells, which were located about a kilometre from the town, had to be re-dug almost daily as they filled quickly with sand. Their slippery sides made drawing water perilous and people sometimes fell in. Walking there and back was an arduous task made easier only for those families who owned a donkey that could be used to haul the load. In most cases it was the women alone who had to bear the heavy burden of the twice-daily trips back and forth to the well - very few indeed could afford the luxury of a donkey.

There were few amenities for women in those days and their lives were very hard. Not only did they have to look after the household and the children, they also cared for the livestock including sheep and camels. They milked the animals, fed the children, received guests and protected their families as well as each other. Of course the women were very close as the communities were small and many people were related either by blood or marriage. They supported and assisted each other whenever they could, so much so in fact that any mother unable to breast-feed her baby could take the child to a neighbour, who would surely help by nursing the child along with her own. Even in the 1940s and 50s, when processed baby food and other modern aids for child rearing were available in the western world, there was no powdered milk or baby formula to be found in the territory of Abu Dhabi, or indeed in the whole of the Gulf.

In addition to caring for the children, the women did everything needed to provide for and sustain the family including sewing the clothes and, if they were near an oasis, even climbing the tall palm trees every day to gather dates for food. They also tended the farms, ploughing the earth, then sowing and watering the seeds, cultivating whatever they grew, and finally harvesting the fruits of their labours. Needless to say they worked from dawn until dusk with little time for leisure - it was a constant uphill struggle with which my mother was quite familiar.

Cooking even the simple foods we ate was also quite a chore because it was done over a wood fire. Before they cooked anything the women first had to find fuel for the fire, not an easy job in a desert environment. They gathered whatever drift wood they could from the sea shore, supplementing it with combustible material they gleaned from the few date palms in the area. They also bought wood from the bedouins who brought it from the desert. Abu Dhabi island itself was barren at the time except for the occasional bush or shrub which was useless as fuel anyway. With the wood they had either gathered or purchased the women made open fires over which they cooked our meals.

Food was scarce and it was often difficult for the men to get sufficient quantities to feed their families but the women were very efficient in making the supplies last for as long as they could. The fare consisted mostly of rice, fish, yogurt and dates. The rice was imported through Dubai from India, fish was caught in the Gulf and the yogurt was made from goat or camel milk. Dates were grown locally but some still had to be shipped in from Bahrain to meet our needs. There was no poultry and very little meat as we kept animals mainly for their milk rather than for slaughter. Liquid refreshments consisted mostly of tea and Arabic coffee. Fresh clean water was still unavailable in Abu Dhabi so we drank the brackish water drawn from the local wells. Thankfully we could avail ourselves of fresh water when we lived in Muwayje during the summers.

We were undernourished for the most part as the milk supply was low and we ate few fruits and vegetables. Such perishable foods, all of which had to be imported, could not survive the long camel trips in the heat. We sometimes used to get pomegranates in season but as there was no refrigeration this was a rare treat. Even the local fish had to be eaten within hours of having been caught so no one ate fish in the evening: it was prepared and eaten at the midday meal because it would not be edible by late afternoon. The people who lived all year round in Al Ain and the Liwa never had fresh fish. Some was dried and taken along when we moved inland for the summer but it was extremely salty and thus not very palatable – we ate it only as a last resort.

Clothing was also as simple as it was scarce. The men usually had a single kandoura or dishdash which they would wash and wear over and over, replacing it only when it was completely worn out. The children wore next to nothing and the women contented themselves with one or two kandouras they had usually stitched themselves. No one had any shoes so we all walked barefoot. Shoes would have been useless in any case. The sand was knee deep and so difficult to navigate that if one wore shoes they only got stuck and buried in the sand and were lost forever after two or three steps.

Because people were poor and had few possessions they tended to share everything with their families, neighbours, and friends. They frequently ate together in the afternoon following the Asr prayer. The men and women gathered in separate groups, usually in the shade of the mosque or someone's home to share whatever they had brought – dates, coffee or something they had cooked over the open fire. If they had a visitor they were very particular about being hospitable and would borrow food from a neighbour if need be, just so they could serve a guest at their home.

There were no hospitals or schools in the 1950s except for the religious school run by Darwish bin Karam, an amazing man who was a teacher, poet, barber, marriage counsellor, imam of the mosque and the community's healer; he also performed circumcisions on all the young boys. While Mulla Darwish did his best to educate the young and care for the sick he was neither a qualified teacher nor a doctor, both of which we needed desperately.

The vast majority of people could not read or write. Illiteracy was probably around 98 per cent. The handful who learned to read did so using the Quran, the only book available to us at the time. Children had no schooling besides reading the Quran in the religious school. As soon as the young boys were twelve or thirteen they would join their fathers, either fishing, pearl diving or tending to the animals to contribute to the family's income. Only a few youngsters were able to pursue their education long enough to learn how to write or to read books besides the Quran.

Other than the herbal medicines prescribed by Mulla Darwish there was no way to treat common ailments, many of which could have been cured with medicines that had been available in the West for decades. Eye infections, for example, were rampant. In the summer tiny mosquitoes would emerge by the thousands, seemingly from nowhere. We were constantly brushing them from our faces, but to no avail. They got in everyone's eyes, particularly those of the children, causing painful infections that sometimes would eventually lead to blindness. There were no medical facilities to speak of: Abu Dhabi's first hospital did not open until 1967. Because there was no clinic or hospital, or even a formally-trained doctor to treat people, the mortality rate was very high and families were much smaller than they are today. Women and children were particularly vulnerable; the mortality rate amongst women was easily thirty per cent at the time. We had only midwives to attend during deliveries so many women died giving birth, including my own mother who was taken from us in 1962 at the age of thirty. Any illness which caused fever was fatal because there was no effective treatment for high temperatures. The traditional herbal medicines we had at our disposal were simply not adequate ammunition against sickness and disease.

It is disappointing that the British, despite their presence in the Trucial States for almost two centuries, never lifted a finger to help us in the areas of education and health care. Not a single brick was laid by the British before 1959 to help the people of Abu Dhabi better their lives; they never built a school, a medical clinic or a mosque.

Since virtually no one could write before 1960 we have no documented historical records of our own. The only things for which we have a record are those which the British Political Agent reported back, along with his personal observations, to the residency in Bushire or Bahrain. Because of this no one but those who were here at the time will ever know our perspective on what happened. Even treaties and agreements were not properly tracked and documents were more often than not misplaced or lost. Because people did not read or write themselves they had little appreciation of books or the importance of preserving written documents and agreements. This put our leaders in the position of having to rely on the other parties in those agreements to keep accurate records of transactions and treaties. Likewise, births, deaths, marriages and the milestones of peoples' lives are not registered anywhere. Most local people born before 1960 can only guess at the year and date of their birth.

Despite the high illiteracy rate, or perhaps because of it, we had a rich oral tradition which included a love of poetry and a deep appreciation of oratory skills. In the days when our people were poorly educated they nevertheless had excellent memories for poetry. Many were able to memorise then recite poems that had been read or told to them only once. There was also a tradition of storytelling in which family histories and knowledge of important events were passed down from one generation to the next. Sadly, with the introduction of mass media to our culture, these skills and traditions are being forgotten and much of our history, even our more recent history, is being lost forever. In the past poetry and storytelling were valued arts as there was little entertainment and very few leisure or cultural activities - we had little dancing or music, for example, other than the traditional drums which were played mostly at marriages to accompany the nuptial dances and songs.

Through the eyes of a child

My early childhood memories of growing up in Abu Dhabi and the Al Ain area are happy ones despite the hardships that surrounded me. Like the majority of youngsters of my age I was blissfully unaware of the difficulties of life in the desert and on the coast of the Arabian Gulf, perhaps even more so as I enjoyed many comforts and privileges that most of my contemporaries did not. My parents had a summer home in Muwayje, near the Al Ain oasis, but I spent the first three or four summers of my life in Sheikh Zayed's palace with him and his wife and their only son Khalifa. The palace was located not too far from my parents' home and my living there helped ease the burden on my mother who had three of us to look after at the time - my elder sister, me and my younger brother - in addition to running the household.

Most of the neighbours in the small village in which we lived were Sheikh Zayed's men, all of whom travelled with him wherever he went leaving the women and children on their own, sometimes for months at a stretch, to manage the affairs of the house and the village in their absence. With me at the palace, and therefore with one less child to manage, my mother was better able to cope with her myriad responsibilities. I, on the other hand, was a welcome companion to Sheikh Khalifa as we were about the same age. Of course I still spent a lot of time in my father's house and I remember the men of the village gathering in our majlis with Sheikh Zayed presiding and everyone contributing to the discussions that went on. Because the settlement was so small everybody knew, respected and cared for one another. We were like one large family to which all in the village belonged. In fact the children had the habit of calling all the adults "aunt" or "uncle" whether they were related to them or not.

After the loss of their parents in 1947, my father and uncles had promised themselves to do their utmost to retain a position in the community and a standard of living of which my grandfather would have been proud. In those days it was very prestigious to keep an open house, receiving guests, being hospitable to visitors and charitable to your neighbours. These were customary practices for the prominent, well-to-do families; people of the community looked up to you if your family was able to maintain this lifestyle. So this is what my father and uncles did, always striving through their hard work to maintain a very good standard of living and a respected position in the community. Each had been either a captain on a boat or an important pearl diver who supplemented his income with trading, shipping and other enterprises in the off-season. With the collapse of the pearl industry they turned to those trading enterprises and new ventures. They worked hard to keep their household going as it was before my grandfather's death: a place in which the mullas and learned men of the community would gather to have an open majlis in which various subjects and problems of the day were discussed. Because there were no radios, newspapers or television the majlis provided a vital communication link where people exchanged information by word of mouth. Those who travelled brought back news from afar and those who learnt or read anything new would enlighten the rest of the majlis. It was a forum for conversation, learning, decision-making and camaraderie for the men of the time. Among those who gathered there I still remember many with great respect: Abdullah bin Misfer, Mohammed bin Sheiban, Saeed Al Badi, Hamed Al Badi, Nasser Bilhall, Ali bin Tarraf, Fahad Al Ahbabi and Yahyeh bin Hassan. All of them lived humble lives in those days, working hard to provide for their families and educate their children. Some are still alive and either they or their sons have gone on to become prominent citizens or high-ranking officials in the government of Abu Dhabi or the UAE.

Unsettled times

Throughout my earliest years my father was frequently away, accompanying Sheikh Zayed on his many trips around the territories that belonged to Abu Dhabi. It was an unsettled time in the region, particularly between 1949 and 1955, when the Saudis once again laid claim to the Buraimi oasis which was within the domain of the Sultanate of Muscat and Oman and bordered on Al Ain where Sheikh Zayed governed. The Saudis supported their claim by supplying and financing the rebels around the area, encouraging them to revolt against the Ruler of Abu Dhabi and the Sultan of Oman both of whom were trying to maintain good relations with the local tribes through ongoing talks and negotiations. Nevertheless there was a lot of friction and conflict. The Saudis were better financed so they had the money and the means to buy the loyalty of the tribal chiefs while the Abu Dhabians had limited resources with which to fight back.

Sheikh Zayed kept in constant communication with the heads of the tribes inhabiting the area, trying to garner support for Abu Dhabi's cause. Unfortunately he did not have the financial means to provide them with what they needed, so all he could do was offer them goodwill, friendship and moral support in times of trouble while trying to convince them to back the ruler of Abu Dhabi in opposing the Saudis' claim to Buraimi. He was also the arbitrator and judge in whatever disputes arose as a result of misunderstandings between the tribes so he was forever on the move from one location to another meeting the tribal chiefs and resolving conflicts. The trips were at least several days long between destinations and Sheikh Zayed and his men travelled by camel, horse or donkey, whichever was available at the time. Of course they were perpetually on the alert and always wore weapons, either guns or swords, to defend themselves in the event of an attack.

Despite his best efforts, however, a lot of the tribes in Al Ain deserted Sheikh Zayed during this period mainly because the Saudis were feeding everybody by cooking huge pots of food and inviting them for daily meals. They were also subsidising the local inhabitants with cash and promising them future support and prosperity. The people in the area, poor and deprived of many of life's essentials, were easily taken in by these promises of plenty. They had gained nothing during 150 years of British domination and felt there was little use in waiting another hundred years in the hopes that the British would finally lend a helping hand. The inhabitants were ripe for change and therefore very receptive to the advances of the Saudis. They had no interest whatsoever in the politics of the area or in what lay beneath the ground, they were more concerned with where their next meal was coming from. All they really wanted was to feed their families and provide a decent standard of living for their children and at the time the Saudis were doing a good job of doling out the meal tickets. That the people of the area should have wavered in their support of Abu Dhabi's cause is perfectly understandable.

As the territorial wrangling intensified the British became more involved in arbitrating between the parties, always, of course, with the ultimate objective of achieving their own goals in the process. At the heart of the territorial dispute was the oil-producing potential of the area. If the Saudis won Buraimi then it would undoubtedly be the American oil companies who would be awarded the concession to explore for oil in all the territory that now lies between Buraimi and the intersection between the borders of the UAE, Oman and Saudi Arabia. If the Omanis and the Abu Dhabians won the fight, on the other hand, then a British company would have a better chance of being granted the concession in that area. Having done the geophysical studies and the preliminary exploration of the possibilities the British knew very well that there was oil and gas there and they had to protect it with every means at their disposal.

The situation came to a head in 1955 when the Trucial Oman Scouts raided the house of the Saudi representative in Hamasa, a village next to Buraimi. They evicted him and all his followers and sent them packing back to Saudi Arabia before handing the town over to the Omani forces.

As a youngster living in Al Ain I witnessed, from a distance, what happened in Hamasa. We heard the noise of gunfire and explosions from our house and we saw the flares and fires as some of the barasti houses went up in flames. We could only thank God that not many people were killed or injured.

The spoils of battle

In the aftermath of the battle, as they cleared the Hamasa and Buraimi area of any remaining Saudi troops, the Trucial Oman Scouts camped between Muwayje and Al Ain at a site close to where the UAE university is situated today. When the clean-up was complete the troops decamped leaving military reminders of their presence behind in the sand. I, and two other village boys my age, walked over to the abandoned camp to scavenge what we could. Much to our delight we discovered an abundance of empty shell boxes, perfect toys and props for the games of three imaginative youths such as ourselves. We gathered as many as we could carry and set off across the dunes for home. It was about a three kilometre walk from the village to the former encampment and the day was hot and dry as usual. It had tired us out just getting there but the real test came on the trek back when our arms were full of the treasured shell boxes - each step seemed more difficult than the last and we grew thirstier by the minute. There we were, three young boys determined to make off with our booty, but the unforgiving desert sun beat down on us and by the half-way mark we were so parched that we were unable to go on.

We might have made it back to the village to cool our parched throats had we left the shell boxes behind, but now that we were the proud owners of such priceless possessions we were unwilling to give them up. We would sooner have died of thirst! So we sat down on the side of a dune with our boxes and waited. Luckily someone saw us from a distance and came to our rescue with a refreshing drink of water thus enabling us to continue on our way without having to leave any of our prizes behind.

As we played with them in the weeks that followed the shell boxes reminded us of what would eventually become known as the "Buraimi incident". Although the actual battle which accompanied the British-backed and locally-supported raid was fairly brief, its impact was long lasting - the area reverted back to the original owners and it remains Omani territory today. Thankfully the casualties were minimal. Only two or three deaths and a few injuries were reported as a result of the raid which finally ended a long period of misunderstanding and tension between Oman, Abu Dhabi, Saudi Arabia, the British and the Americans. Naturally the local inhabitants were pleased to see the end of the conflict, particularly since it had been their prodding which had pushed the British to act using the Trucial Oman Scouts.

A young life lost

Shortly after the Buraimi incident my family was devastated by a tragic accident. One morning, my younger brother, who was about six years old at the time, was playing in the courtyard of our house with our three and a half-year-old sister. He found a small box full of unused matches which he began lighting and throwing on the ground. My little sister, anxious to join in the game, went over to retrieve one of the matches and as she bent over her dress brushed against the flame and caught fire. She was badly burnt in a matter of minutes. Unfortunately there were no doctors, nurses, or medicine for treating anything - let alone burns - in Muwayje; nor were there any medical facilities in nearby Al Ain or Buraimi. The nearest medical clinic was in Sharjah, and that was at least a two-day journey away. The whole family was distraught, my little sister was in excruciating pain and there was nothing we could do to alleviate her suffering.

Concerned for my sister's welfare, Sheikh Zayed kindly lent my father his Land Rover and a driver to take us to Sharjah. The RAF, which was using an airport there, had a medical facility – the only such facility in the whole area at the time. My father and mother, myself and my other siblings all got into the Land Rover with my injured sister and headed across the desert from Al Ain to Sharjah. Of course there was no road other than a sandy track that followed the route of the camel caravans so we got stuck many times along the way and the adults had to get out and push the vehicle. It took us two days to cover a distance that can now be travelled in a couple of hours at most. By the time we arrived in Sharjah it was too late; my little sister had already died from the burns.

It was an unfortunate accident. But equally unfortunate, and completely unforgivable, was the fact that as late as 1957 there was not a single doctor in the Sheikhdom of Abu Dhabi. Most of the rest of the world had easy access to doctors, medicine, and the latest in medical technology to treat the injured and ill. We, on the other hand, had nothing, not even the simplest and most basic medical services. As a result my family lost a beautiful young child, and before her my grandfather and grandmother, when all three might have been saved had there been medical facilities here at the time. Our family was not the only one to be touched by such tragedies – many people died or suffered needlessly because of the lack of proper medical care in Abu Dhabi and across the Trucial States. Sadly these facilities could have easily been provided had there been a will to do so. But it was only in 1961 that the first missionary clinic was established in Al Ain and not until 1967 that a hospital was finally built in Abu Dhabi.

Entrepreneurial spirit
My whole family was badly shaken by the loss of my little sister, but, as it always does, life went on. My father settled down to a more normal routine than the one he had been leading prior to the Buraimi incident when he was moving from one tribal area to another with Sheikh Zayed trying to muster support against the Saudis. Now that his life was a little more sedentary he decided to open a shop, a small general store which stocked food and textiles, in the village where we lived. He got his older brother, my uncle, to tend the shop. Unfortunately my uncle could neither read nor write. Undaunted by this handicap he gave credit to the shop customers and tracked the amounts owing by placing coffee beans beside their names – which he had cleverly managed to memorise. When my

father returned from his trips with Sheikh Zayed my uncle would tell him what each customer owed based on the number of coffee beans placed beside the names on the ledger. It was a system that was to prove more to the benefit of the customers than to my father the shop owner. Within about a year he was forced to close the business partly because he could not trace the creditors: my uncle had a lot of coffee beans but not many identifiable clients and even less cash!

Besides my uncle's creative accounting methods, the extreme poverty in the area contributed to the failure of my father's shop in Muwayje - people simply did not have any money to pay for what they needed to live. The best they could do was to barter goods and services in exchange for supplies from the shop as there was little currency or cash circulating in the community. While rumours spread about the possibility of crude oil being found in commercial quantities in Abu Dhabi, people were at the end of their tether and many were hardly able to survive. They needed to earn an income and all they had to live off were the farms in Al Ain as Abu Dhabi had nothing to offer them at the time.

Although we continued to spend the winters in Abu Dhabi, we moved our summer home from Muwayje to Al Ain shortly after the death of my little sister. Al Ain was becoming more prominent among the seven or so villages of the Buraimi oasis. A small souk had been built there by Sheikh Zayed and people from the environs came to trade animal skins and agricultural produce - such as mangoes, dates and oil - for staple foods and textile goods. Some even travelled from the interior of Oman to barter and trade. Because the souk was busy my father decided to open another shop, this time with his other brother Ahmed, but he did not limit himself to that business alone.

Even in his younger years my father was an entrepreneur and an adventurer, always willing to try new things. He never worried about failing, which he did on occasion, because he felt the most important thing was to try - if he succeeded, so much the better. As he witnessed the arrival of more and more trucks and four-wheel drive vehicles in Abu Dhabi he recognised an opportunity to offer transportation services for goods and people between Abu Dhabi, Dubai and Al Ain. In keeping with his entrepreneurial spirit he bought himself an old second-hand truck, hired a driver and went into the transportation business. He did not drive the truck himself but often went along for the ride which he enjoyed. Later, he bought an old 1952 Chevrolet pick-up which he drove personally. He would sometimes follow the transport truck with the pick-up in a two vehicle convoy - if the former broke down the latter was right behind to provide assistance. The business did well initially but the old vehicles soon began to break down more frequently, as might be expected with the lack of roads and the harsh desert conditions under which they were being driven. There was a general shortage of replacement parts for trucks of any kind, while maintenance and repair services were virtually non-existent. As a result the condition of the vehicles went from bad to worse. When he did manage to get them fixed, the repairs would often cost more that the freight charges for a trip. Needless to say the whole venture folded abruptly after about a year when both trucks broke down in the desert between Al Ain and Abu Dhabi - they may yet lie rusting quietly in some sandy grave beneath a dune. The irony is that their final resting place is not far from where my grandfather was buried in 1947, ten years before the first motorised vehicle arrived in Abu Dhabi.

In addition to his commercial ventures my father stayed very much involved with Sheikh Zayed. He accompanied him whenever he travelled, a constant companion and one of his closest advisors. When Sheikh Zayed settled down in Al Ain for any length of time my father occupied himself with one business or another but in the end his priority was meeting Sheikh Zayed's needs and helping him whenever he could.

Sheikh Zayed was always loved and respected by all who knew him, from his friends and counsellors to the smallest child. When the first electrical generator was installed in his Al Ain palace he endeared himself to every child in the village by using it to show films (or rather a film, an Egyptian Arabic film called The Black Knight), to all who wished to watch. He hosted a makeshift open-air theatre by projecting the film onto one of the palace walls - much like a drive-in without the cars. All the village inhabitants sat in the sand, completely mesmerised by the events on the big "screen" in front of us; Sheikh Zayed was always somewhere in our midst. It was wonderful. Not one of us cared that we only had one film, which we knew by heart after several showings. We watched it over and over until we could have played the parts ourselves because seeing a film, even after the hundredth showing, was still a novelty in those days.

Early school days with Mulla Darwish

From about 1956 onwards, when we were in Abu Dhabi, both my older sister and I attended the religious school run by Darwish bin Karam, the village teacher, poet, barber, healer and mulla. The school day started early, about 6.00 a.m., and lasted until noon with an hour-long breakfast break between eight and nine. I remember being so excited about going to school that I would sleep fully dressed so as not to waste any time with preparations in the morning. As soon as I awoke, I was up, out of the house and on my way. My sister and I often raced each other and the neighbouring boys to see who would get there first. It was not uncommon for us to arrive at the school before the mulla had finished the morning prayer at about 4.30 a.m.

I kept this up for a long time: it was a delightful game that added a little excitement to otherwise routine days. One morning, however, as I was running to school, I heard disturbing sounds from one of the houses on the way. Curiosity got the better of me and I stopped to investigate. When I entered the house to take a look I came upon a scene I shall never forget. There were women wailing and men gathered round - it seemed as if an accident had occurred. I looked more closely and saw a man lying on the ground. As I listened to the shouting around me I learned what had happened.

There was an Iraqi mason who had an old man as a helper. The two were on their way to work when they had a disagreement. The mason got so angry that he picked up a shovel and struck the old man on the head, killing him with the blow. The sight of the old man drenched in blood and the mason being held by the neighbours while everyone was screaming, shouting and crying scared the life out of me - so much so in fact that it was the last time I ventured out alone before sunrise. But despite the fright I continued to go to school.

Like the houses in Abu Dhabi town the school was built of palm fronds, a round, one-roomed shelter with a pitched roof. Of course it had no equipment, teaching aids, sanitary facilities or water. Each morning before instruction began we had to replenish a big water container inside the school. We did so by filling small jugs at the well - which was about half a kilometre away - carrying them back to the school, then dumping them into the container until we had enough water - brackish though it was - to last us through the morning. Despite these primitive amenities and the lack of educational tools, Mulla Darwish bin Karam did an admirable job of instructing the village children.

His teaching style was simple. He would position himself in the middle of the room facing the door while we, the pupils, sat in the sand or on woven mats in a circle around him. Twenty-five or thirty of us, both boys and girls, sat silently reading, each of us struggling over a different page of the Quran. In fact, our entire education consisted solely of reading the Holy Book. We read it in its entirety, one page at a time, a slow and painful process for some of the less clever students. When we felt confident in our ability to tackle any given page Mulla Darwish would listen to us reading it aloud. Once he was satisfied with our performance, he allowed us to go on to the next page. There was no question of progressing to a new page until we had completely mastered the one which preceded it. When he had his hands full the mulla sometimes designated the older boys to listen to the younger ones and help them along. While most of us progressed at a reasonable pace, some students would stay stuck on the same page for days at a time. Even the sharpest among us took at least a couple of years to go through the Quran in its entirety. It was a lengthy procedure. I do not recall anyone completing it in a single school year which normally began in October and ended in May.

Every time a student finished reading the Quran we would all dress up and pass through the town chanting and singing in celebration. People would give us sweets, or sometimes even a quarter of a rupee or half a rupee for the teacher. It was a big day when any of the students finished the Quran and thereby graduated from the school. The only other highlight of the school year was when the rains came in winter. As soon as the rain began to fall, our concentration was broken. We knew it would soon mean the closing of the school because of flooding. More often than not, within two or three days of the rain having stopped, the shelter would be full of water and unfit for students. The brief holiday which ensued was a welcome break from the six day a week routine of reading for several hours each morning.

The mulla was compensated for his work based on the number of students he taught. He was supposed to be paid a quarter of a rupee per student per week but many of the students could not afford to pay even that small amount. He taught them nevertheless, telling them to bring the money when they could. The more financially able students however, would pay a rupee every two weeks. In addition, when his or her education was complete, each student was to donate two rupees to the mulla. Despite the small payment in relation to the services rendered many could not manage this token donation either, so they paid only a portion of the graduation gratuity to the teacher.

After completing this part of their education – and for most this was the only formal education they received – some continued with the mulla to learn how to write. The method by which we learned this new skill was no more inspiring than the way we were taught to read – we did it by copying. The teacher wrote a sentence at the top of a page; we copied it over and over until our sheet was filled. As one's skills improved Mulla Darwish might write a composition for copying, which at least helped to break the monotony. Those of us who were fortunate enough to pursue our education, tedious though it may have been at times, were very grateful for the opportunity to do so. Most of our playmates and compatriots were denied an education; because their families were very poor, even the children had to work. At the age of twelve the boys started as apprentices with their fathers, learning to either fish, farm or tend to the livestock.

Six-room schoolhouse

In 1959 the British government built a small building which they subsequently gave to Sheikh Shakhbut to be used as a school. By that time there were about fifty of us, both boys and girls, being taught the Quran by Mulla Darwish in the barasti shelter which had served as our school until then. Regrettably, the new six-room building was not much of an improvement over the barasti hut, apart from the fact that it had solid walls and a roof, and even these proved to be disadvantageous in the intense heat of the late spring and early autumn. The building was outfitted with the most basic equipment – desks, chairs and chalkboards – but little else. There was no water (we brought our own from home), no sanitary facilities (we used the sea and the beach), no electricity, no educational tools and only one teacher for all of us despite the fact that we were now going to be divided into three separate "classrooms". Of course there were no text books, save one for the teacher, and we all had to purchase our own exercise books and pencils from the souk. It was several years before the Ruler imported text books from Jordan and provided us with much needed school supplies.

At the new school we were expected to arrive and leave at set times unlike the Quranic school where we came and went as we pleased. The school term was also longer. We started earlier in the autumn, in September, and went right through until June which meant we suffered the heat and humidity more at the beginning and the end of the school year. In addition, attendance was taken every day and we were punished if we were absent. At the Quranic school nobody had bothered to take attendance or find out why we had failed to make an appearance if we were absent. If we told the mulla we had a stomach ache and had to drink haloul, a herbal medicine to clear the system, we could take our leave. In the new school, however, having to take herbal medicine was not a valid excuse for being absent. Although there was more discipline than we had been accustomed to it was not enough to make the school a real educational institution.

Mulla Darwish retired from teaching when the new school opened. He became general secretary to the Ruler and kept busy writing letters, issuing passports and looking after the Ruler's interests. Ahmed Al Khatib, a Palestinian who had been living in Jordan, was his unfortunate replacement. On the first day of school he lined us all up one behind the other to determine our ages and names so he could separate us into three groups – one group per classroom. We tried our best to cooperate but none of us knew our ages and many of us did not know our full names, we knew only those by which our families and friends called us. Nobody had ever asked our full names before. We were totally perplexed about how best to answer his questions. Because of the confusion we ended up being called by all kinds of different names and titles most of which had to be changed in later years to reflect our ancestry accurately. Whenever I think of that incident it serves to remind me of just how simple and naive we all were at the time. We finally ended up being grouped, not by age, but by our ability to read, write or identify letters.

Each group was assigned to one of the three classrooms between which the teacher shuttled throughout the day trying to manage all the pupils and teach them something at the same time – an almost impossible task further complicated by the lack of text books. Nevertheless he did his best. He would extract sentences and passages from the single book he had, writing them on the board for us to copy. Those of us who could write would scratch away in our exercise books as long as he was in the room then abandon our work for horseplay as soon as he left to attend to another class. Needless to say we did not learn much during our first year there. Year two was no better as we still did not have any text books and there continued to be a shortage of supplies and equipment.

While we students suffered from the paucity of school supplies, the teacher lived without even the most basic amenities. I am quite sure he wondered why he had been invited to Abu Dhabi to teach. Nobody supported him in his efforts. Worse yet, no one even bothered to provide him with a place to live. He had to sleep in one of the empty rooms at the schoolhouse because there were no other available lodgings. Of course he had no sanitary facilities or water and so, like us, he had to make do. On top of all that, food was scarce as well. Whichever way he turned he faced an uphill struggle to live, to understand the situation here and to try teaching almost completely illiterate youngsters. In looking back, I am surprised he lasted a year let alone two! He would never have stayed as long as he did without a tremendous amount of determination and sacrifice – anyone else would have packed up and left because it was such an unworkable situation.

The lack of facilities and sufficient instructors, while tragic, was certainly understandable given the times and the attitude many local people had toward education. Most were more concerned about making ends meet than about sending their children to school. The Ruler himself placed little importance on education and saw no reason to upgrade or expand the facilities we had in 1959. When we moved into the new building he questioned the need for additional teachers saying the mulla had managed quite well on his own for many years. Why, he asked, was there suddenly a requirement for more than one teacher? It took a lot of effort and convincing by those who believed in education as a stepping stone to the future to persuade the Ruler that we needed three separate teachers because we were in three separate classrooms. It was simply impossible for one person alone to do the job and do it well.

The British, on the other hand, might have encouraged education of the local population had it furthered their own interests to do so. However, it was not until later, when British companies found they needed locally trained and educated workers, that the oil companies became more involved in establishing training facilities of their own - thus the opening of the Abu Dhabi Marine Areas (ADMA) industrial training school, set up in 1960 to teach students job-related skills required to work in the oil fields. The new training school drew a lot of boys from the regular school, taught them the fundamentals of oil field work for a few months, during which they were paid a salary, then sent them to work on Das Island or inland at the oil installations. In either case, they were paid poorly. The schools were later taken over by the government and mostly closed down because they were initially opened to meet the labour needs of the foreign oil companies rather than the educational requirements of the local people. As they folded, other educational and training facilities opened to take their place.

The students who were left behind in the small British built schoolhouse - supposedly run and supported by the Ruler - had an incomplete education because of the lack of teachers, tools and equipment. It would be many years before the young people of Abu Dhabi would get a decent education.

Good intentions

In 1959, the year the six-room schoolhouse was built, there was a terrible flood. A violent storm hit, washing the sea over the village of Abu Dhabi which was not protected by the Corniche as it is today. There was nothing to prevent the high seas, which reached four or five feet, from flooding the town. The storm blew in during the night as people slept thus catching everyone unaware. We all scrambled trying to salvage what we could but it happened so fast that not much could be saved. In no time the water level in the souk was more than three feet high, so deep that we had to fashion makeshift boats by cutting large oil barrels in half to get from one place to another. Every single household in Abu Dhabi - from where the Sheraton Hotel now sits to the present day site of the British

Embassy compound – was severely damaged. The only structures which were spared were the Ruler's palace and a few surrounding houses which stood on relatively high ground. The waters did not recede for two days during which we paddled around either in the halved oil drums or small canoes.

About a week after the flood a large British ship anchored not far from shore and unloaded some dry blankets and canned food which were distributed from the back of a truck to the inhabitants of the town. It was a kind and much appreciated gesture. We were particularly grateful for the dry blankets as most of ours had either been washed away or had become completely soaked with sea water. The canned food, however, was received somewhat less enthusiastically. None of us had eaten canned goods before and we were unsure of what the tins contained. Should it be cooked or eaten straight from the container? None of us knew for sure. There was English writing on the side of the cans but no one could read it. Despite the good intentions with which it was supplied the canned food was never consumed; we were, however, very thankful for the warm blankets on the cool winter nights which followed the flood.

Chapter 4

Mixed Blessings

Black gold

Without the development of the oil industry it is unlikely that the
Abu Dhabi of today would look any different from the Abu Dhabi of
one hundred years ago. Virtually everything we have has been built
with the proceeds generated by the extraction of this valuable natural
resource - so valuable in fact, that it is often referred to as "black
gold." Because of its importance, the milestones in the evolution of
this vital industry in the Gulf region generally, and in Abu Dhabi in
particular, are fairly well known. Various sources, including oil
company publications, detail its history with a wealth of relevant
information.

Oil was a factor in the economics and the politics of the Gulf
region long before it became central to the development of Abu
Dhabi. The first oil concession in the region was awarded to the
Turkish Petroleum Company in 1903. Before the first world war
several countries had competed in the Middle East, mostly in Iraq,
for oil concessions. The Ottomans, however, dominated the area
until the collapse of their empire in 1918. Subsequently, the British,
the French and the Americans divided the Ottoman dominion,
challenging them over the Middle East territories. Oil was in big
demand both during and after the war; it became a race between
nations to see who would be first to conclude successfully
negotiations for the region's key concessions. The British, Americans
and French all felt certain that the Gulf region had extensive deposits
of oil so they competed fiercely to sew up concession agreements
with the rulers, kings and sheikhs throughout the area. In 1927,
BAPCO, an American company, was awarded a concession in
Bahrain. In 1933 SOCAL was granted its first concession in Saudi
Arabia, then British Petroleum (BP) and Gulf Oil were later awarded
concessions in Kuwait in 1934.

As international competition for oil resources heated up, the
British cleverly re-confirmed the agreements they had signed with
the Trucial States sheikhs in 1892 prohibiting communication with
other foreign countries. The sheikhs agreed not to give oil
concessions or lease any territory to any foreigner without the prior
consent and approval of the British. In 1935, Petroleum Concessions

Ltd (PCL), a subsidiary of the London based Iraq Petroleum Company, established an office in Bahrain to handle concession agreements in the region. In 1936, PCL created Petroleum Development (Trucial Coast) - PD(TC) - a joint venture between various large international oil companies.

That same year, most of the Trucial sheikhs, including Sheikh Shakhbut, signed oil exploration options which paved the way for the concession agreements which would follow. With the proceeds Sheikh Shakhbut was able to provide much-needed employment to local inhabitants for about four years.

Shortly after the options were secured, PD(TC) approached the sheikhs with concession agreements granting the company exclusive rights to explore for oil in their respective territories. The Ruler of Dubai was the first to grant a concession in May 1937; he was followed by the Ruler of Sharjah who signed an agreement in September of the same year. In December of the following year PD(TC), which would eventually become the Abu Dhabi Company for Onshore Oil Operations (ADCO), signed agreements with the Rulers of Ras al Khaimah and Kalba. Knowing the terms of SOCAL's agreement with the Saudis and the BAPCO agreement with the Bahrainis, the Ruler of Abu Dhabi held out a little longer for more favourable terms and conditions. After trying to negotiate a better deal he ended by penning an agreement in January 1939 in which he got 300,000 Indian rupees for signing the concession (the equivalent of approximately 300,000 dirhams), 100,000 rupees yearly during the exploration phase, then 200,000 rupees yearly once oil was found in commercial quantities and an additional three rupees on every tonne that was exported. The agreement was to cover a period of seventy-five years.

The outbreak of the second world war in 1939 deferred further oil exploration activities until 1946 after the war had ended. Three years later the first exploratory well was drilled at Ras Sadr, about fifty kilometres from Abu Dhabi island on the way to Dubai; a power station and a desalination plant have since been built there. After more than a year of drilling, the well was determined to be dry and was abandoned in the spring of 1951. The sheikhdom's second well was drilled at Murban, about 100 kilometres south-west of Abu Dhabi island. It, and several others in different locations, were also abandoned before drillers returned to Murban in 1958 where they finally found commercial quantities of oil the following year.

In the meantime, another concession in Abu Dhabi's coastal waters had been awarded by Sheikh Shakhbut in 1953. Abu Dhabi Marine Areas (ADMA) - a company formerly owned by British Petroleum and TOTAL - was formed to explore and exploit the offshore reserves. ADMA headquartered its exploration activities at Das Island, a small, previously uninhabited island about sixty kilometres from mainland Abu Dhabi. Almost overnight, the place was transformed from a barren strip of land to a busy oil camp which supported the company's efforts in the area. The marine surveying, which was even more complex than prospecting on land, included contracting the services of the world famous underwater explorer Jacques Cousteau. The intense and costly efforts paid off relatively quickly. Oil was struck in the seabed concession in 1958. The first shipment left Das Island four years later in July 1962. Eighteen months later, in December 1963, the first shipment from the onshore field at Bab was exported from Jebel Dhanna. Although the early years of the oil industry were very successful from a technical and commercial standpoint, they were not without difficulties for the people of Abu Dhabi.

Empty promises

With the decline of the pearl industry from the early 1930s onwards the situation had grown increasingly desperate in the sheikhdom. The construction of the Ruler's palace had provided a short term respite from the chronic unemployment and widespread poverty but the early forties found Abu Dhabians worse off than they had ever been. When exploration then drilling began in the latter part of the decade things finally started looking up. With the discovery of oil in commercial quantities ten years later, there seemed finally to be a light at the end of the tunnel. Contrary to what many people think, however, the early days of the oil industry were only marginally better than the decades of poverty which had preceded them.

Local people employed by the oil companies earned a meagre living. None got rich. Nor were they encouraged to work for the companies as suppliers or contractors as had happened in Saudi Arabia where the locals were assisted in establishing their own oil field supply and contracting companies. In fact, in Abu Dhabi the opposite was true. The oil companies discouraged the locals from participating in any way other than as hired hands. The people who worked for the oil companies during the 1950s and early 1960s look back with bitterness rather than fondness on those early days. Many have since become prominent citizens; some are ministers or ambassadors, others are highly qualified people in their respective professions. The painful memories of their exploitation, however, linger on even today. While they may have forgiven, they can never forget.

As exploration activities picked up again after the war, more and more local people found employment with the oil companies.

Grateful for the opportunity to work and support their families they took any job that was offered. Most were manual labourers such as sweepers, watchmen, drivers and cooks. The better jobs, however, seemed inevitably to go to Indians or Arab expatriates from Lebanon, Syria and Palestine. While the expatriates supervised, the locals performed the hard labour for which they were often paid less than three rupees per day. Labourers doing similar work in Saudi Arabia and Kuwait, by comparison, were making about five times that amount. In addition to the pay inequities, the local workers suffered inferior accommodation as well as poor food and sub-standard working conditions. Life in the camps was more than tolerable for the well-treated expatriates however. They rested comfortably in prefabricated housing, enjoying nutritious meals of meat, fish and vegetables. The local labourers, on the other hand, slept either in tents, if they were lucky, or under the stars if they were not, and were fed little more than a subsistence diet consisting mainly of rice and lentils.

Workers were given one month's leave after the completion of one year's service. Those fortunate enough to live in Tarif - a distance of about sixty kilometres - might visit their families at the weekend because they were located close to home. However, many could not afford the travel-related costs as transportation was not supplied by the oil company at the time. Those who lived and worked on Das Island were always separated from their families for long periods as there was no chance of travelling back and forth between the mainland and the island unless it was for annual leave or an emergency. For people whose lives revolved around their families this was an extreme hardship.

In addition, the locals' opportunities for promotion within the oil industry were virtually non-existent. Anyone who got a job stayed in whatever position he was hired into for a very long time, if not forever. The promise of the oil industry proved empty for Abu Dhabians, at least in the early stages. They were underpaid, treated poorly, denied opportunities and made to work in very harsh conditions.

Consequently there was always friction between the local workers and the company supervisors. The ill feelings sometimes even spilled over into relations with the local bedouin people who lived near the company camps. One story is told of some bedouin who went to one of the camps to ask for a handout. The camp supervisors refused to share their food, chasing the bedouin away with shouts and threats, telling them never to return. That night, as the supervisors slept soundly in their tent, the bedouin crept back to the camp. The next morning the supervisors were awoken unusually early as they found themselves without a tent to shield their eyes from the sharp rays of the morning sun. The hungry desert dwellers were so quick, quiet and skilful in spiriting the tent away that the supervisors slept straight through until sunrise before they knew their shelter was gone. They all awoke with a fright believing that evil jinn must have somehow stolen their tent in the night. On that occasion at least, the locals had the last laugh.

Innocent pranks, however, may only have worsened the situation. When the workers tried to get more pay and better working conditions, they were either totally dismissed or jailed. It was a dismal situation in many respects, one which eventually pushed the workers to strike in 1963.

Three years later, when Sheikh Zayed became the Ruler of Abu Dhabi, one of his first acts was to renegotiate the concession agreements with the oil companies thus improving the terms and conditions. He also pressured them to purchase locally instead of importing supplies from Europe. From then on things began to turn around. The relationship between the foreign oil interests and local entrepreneurs improved substantially, eventually blossoming into a mutually beneficial association which laid the foundation for the thriving economy in Abu Dhabi today. Now, the Government of Abu Dhabi, through the ADNOC Group of Companies, holds the controlling interest in the Emirate's oil industry. All the companies in the ADNOC Group are committed to the nationalisation of the workforce, particularly at senior management levels, through the ongoing professional development and training of UAE nationals. Policies such as these are providing an environment in which Abu Dhabians can make ever greater contributions to the progress of the oil industry, the Emirate and the country.

The future looks brighter

As the oil industry began to expand in the late 1950s, so did the relative importance of Abu Dhabi town as a trading and commercial centre. Also within the Sheikhdom of Abu Dhabi, Al Ain was growing in leaps and bounds under the patronage of Sheikh Zayed. In some areas it had even outstripped Abu Dhabi town in its development. Sheikh Zayed was so keen on seeing the Al Ain area flourish that he borrowed money, relying on the goodwill of his supporters to finance projects which he felt were important to the future of the area. While my father was fond of Al Ain and supported Sheikh Zayed in his efforts, he felt his own future lay on the island of Abu Dhabi. In anticipation of the opportunities he saw arising as a result of the oil industry he had moved his stock and shop here in 1959. In the early 1960s we continued to spend most of the year on the island, moving inland to Al Ain from May until October. By then we usually travelled in the back of trucks, leaving Abu Dhabi in the late afternoon and arriving in Al Ain around mid-morning the following day after spending a night beside a dune along the way. Our lives were in a constant state of flux with the shifting back and forth between one place and the other but the moves made the weather bearable especially for the very young and the very old.

While we continued to migrate in the spring and the autumn the number of people who remained on Abu Dhabi island throughout the year began increasing along with the growing importance of the oil industry. Because there is no reliable census information for any of the Trucial States until very recently, however, the exact population of Abu Dhabi at the time is unknown. It was estimated to be around 1,500 in Abu Dhabi town in 1950, having declined from a peak of near 3,000 at the turn of the century. However the local population was still quite small in the early 1960s, many people having left to seek better prospects elsewhere. It was gauged more accurately when a smallpox epidemic broke out in Dubai in January and February 1962. To prevent further spread of the disease the British brought in a two-person medical team to inoculate as many people as they could in the Sheikhdom of Abu Dhabi. An estimated ninety per cent of the total population in Abu Dhabi town (3,564) and the Al Ain/Buraimi area (5,000) was inoculated. The inhabitants of the Liwa, who were not inoculated, were believed to be about 3,000 in number, bringing the total population of the entire sheikhdom to around 13,000, a third of which would have been employable men.

While the local population was increasing slowly, the influx of foreigners was climbing comparatively quickly and it was becoming quite evident that Abu Dhabi needed to develop at a much faster pace than it was. Almost daily, the oil companies brought in more people - many of them workers from the subcontinent. There were no restaurants to feed the foreigners, nor was there housing to accommodate them. We did not even have a hotel in Abu Dhabi at the time. The Ruler and government were not yet channelling the oil revenues through the economy so people had to borrow from each other to build small rooms and restaurants to cope with the demand. Although the Ruler approved plans for a hotel in 1961 it was not ready to receive guests until the autumn of 1962.

For the most part, the inhabitants here welcomed the arrival of expatriates. They saw the newcomers as a sign of economic growth and as a source of employment which could only better their standard of living. The local people took advantage of the influx however they could. Some Abu Dhabians rented parts of their homes. Others managed to buy the odd car or pick-up and lease them to the foreign companies. The local people tried to accommodate the foreigners because their presence meant prosperity and brighter prospects for the future. They did not, on the other hand, take advantage of the situation by overcharging for products or services, although they very easily could have. Rather, they dealt with the expatriates with extraordinary goodwill and the most honourable intentions, generating a modest income for themselves while fulfilling the visitors' needs as best they could.

Daring desert driving

Despite the snail's pace at which it was moving, progress was nevertheless pulling us ever so slowly into the future, though sometimes the directions in which it took us seemed oddly disjointed, even comical as I look back on it now. Motorised vehicles – mostly ex-army trucks and four-wheel drives – had begun to appear in the sheikhdom in the late 1950s. Their popularity grew, particularly with members of the ruling family who were more able to afford them at the time. As incomes rose and the vehicles became less expensive, more people bought them even though we still had no roads. Very gradually, transportation by camel, horse and donkey became less common. Those who owned motorised vehicles drove them anywhere and everywhere – between the narrow passages that separated the houses, willy nilly across the desert, along the beach – wherever their hearts desired. As they drove, they turned and swerved haphazardly to avoid getting stuck in the sand. The evidence of these early driving habits can be seen in old photographs where tyre tracks criss cross in a million different directions looking somehow out of place amidst the clutch of barasti houses and the wide expanse of sand.

Not long after the first four-wheel drive vehicles arrived, saloon cars were imported for the ruler and some members of his family. While the four-wheel drives sometimes had difficulty navigating in the soft sand the saloon cars invariably got stuck wherever they went. My most vivid memories of the first saloon cars are of them being pushed around the palace by the Ruler's guards. The Ruler himself was usually forced to join in the effort and the only one who got any pleasure from the outings was the driver, Mohammed Al Khurashi, who remained in the car to steer while everybody else pushed and shoved. Al Khurashi was Sheikh Shakhbut's driver from the day the Ruler's first car arrived in the late 1940s until Sheikh Shakhbut died in 1990. In fact the loyal driver died shortly after the man whom he had chauffeured for over four decades.

In recalling the driving conditions of the time, Sir Bernard

Burrows, the first political resident in the Persian Gulf, referred to the difficulties of driving on the island:

> "It would surprise visitors to today's Abu Dhabi to know that the approaches to that town were, in my day, quite hazardous owing to muddy areas near the coast in which it was easy to get stuck; indeed once when we were travelling from the Political Agency the short distance of a few hundred yards to the Ruler's mud-brick palace, our Land Rover got stuck in the sand and we had to call in the local inhabitants to push us out in order not to make too dishevelled an appearance at the Ruler's reception."[1]

It was easier to drive in the desert. The ground was harder there than on the island of Abu Dhabi where the sand was soft and deep, although all vehicles had to be equipped with special balloon sand tyres to enable them to move at all. Once a vehicle got bogged down it was tough to get it out. Most drivers carried corrugated metal sheets or steel plates as well as shovels, the former to put under the wheels and the latter to dig themselves out with when they got stuck. Although there was no road from the town to the edge of the island until 1961, there was a causeway at Maqta from 1952 onwards. It was made of stone and mud and stood about two feet above water level so both cars and camels could easily cross the channel. Prior to the construction of the causeway camel caravans had to wait, sometimes for hours, for low tide before they could make their way onto the island from the mainland. The channel crossing was an inconvenience to residents but it was also a deterrent to intruders. It was this natural defence that initially made Abu Dhabi attractive as a settlement site. The guard tower that was used to watch the shallow part of the channel still stands today, completely reconstructed, near where the first Maqta bridge was built in 1968.

Though still very young at the time I was fascinated by the motorised vehicles and was itching to learn how to drive. I saw an opportunity to do so by exploiting the laziness of one of my relatives, a twenty-three year old cousin in Al Ain who owned a vehicle. He had purchased a Land Rover for his own use but soon found himself saddled with some unwanted chores. Because he was the only one in the family with transportation he was expected to rise very early in the morning, go with the farmer to the date palm grove, gather the dates required for the day and bring them back to the village before seven o'clock in the morning. My cousin, who much preferred his sleep to this pre-dawn trip, was quite happy to relinquish his car and

(1) Burrows, B.; "Footnotes in the Sand - The Gulf in Transition, 1953 - 1958"; Michael Russell (Publishing) Ltd.; Salisbury.

allow me to perform this early morning chore for him. Unfortunately he refused categorically to let me drive, or even set foot in the car, after sunrise. While he slept I was free to take the Land Rover at will but as soon as he awoke I had to surrender the privilege until the next morning. Nevertheless, I have him to thank for allowing me to learn how to drive at the tender age of thirteen!

Just as there were no roads in Abu Dhabi, so it was in Al Ain. People drove through the alleyways and between the houses and date palm groves where there were sometimes rough tracks to follow. If there was such a track we drove on the left-hand side of it as the British still do. Since the British drove on the left-hand side of the tracks the local people who acquired vehicles simply followed suit. There were few vehicles, no need to register them and therefore no licence plates; but we all knew which vehicles belonged to whom by the colour, make and model.

Petrol, imported from Abadan in Iran, was shipped in by tug boat, off-loaded in Dubai, then distributed throughout the Trucial States, including Abu Dhabi, by truck. Most of the petroleum products we received in the early 1960s were supplied by British Petroleum (BP). The petrol was made available in the villages through a local representative, usually a shop owner whose business faced onto a track or bordered an open area. It arrived in big barrels so the shop owner would be provided with a hand pump to transfer it from the barrels into the vehicles. The local distributors were paid a maintenance fee by the oil company for selling the petrol to the vehicle owners.

Heaven on earth

In another transportation-related development in the early 1960s, airline routes were established between Abu Dhabi and Sharjah and Abu Dhabi and Bahrain by Gulf Aviation, the forerunner of Gulf Air. Dakotas and Hurons, old second world war planes which carried eight to twelve passengers, were pressed into service on the first regularly scheduled flights in and out of Abu Dhabi. They were very noisy aircraft which often caused passengers to suffer headaches from the constant roar of the engines. Nevertheless the flights were always full. It was an ongoing struggle to make a reservation let alone board the planes that took off and landed from a stretch of sabkha, or salt flat, which served as Abu Dhabi's airport at the time. While airports around the world were installing the latest in aviation technology we did our best to provide the most basic requirement – a landing strip. Two labourers were charged with the frequent spraying of a kilometre-long section of sabkha to keep it compacted and hard thus allowing the planes to land with relative ease. Despite this imaginative runway maintenance system the aircraft occasionally got stuck in the soft sand. When they did, every donkey and able-bodied man in town was mustered at the airstrip to extricate the plane. This procedure was a sight to behold – such a juxtaposition of the old and the new as the hundred or so donkeys and all available hands tried to pull the plane free.

I experienced the same meeting of the ancient and the modern when I took my first trip beyond the shores of mainland Abu Dhabi in 1961.

Two of my uncles, Abdul Rahim and Abdul Hakim, lived and worked on Das Island. The former, who had captained a dhow owned by Al Yousef, had moved to Das Island several years earlier when he became part-owner of the island's canteen. He lived there permanently, returning to visit Abu Dhabi every six or eight months when he could manage the time away. The second uncle, who had tracked the customers' debts with coffee beans at my father's shop in Muwayje, also worked and lived on the island. My first solo adventure away from home was a visit to the two of them on Das Island.

I left Abu Dhabi in a dhow one afternoon, travelled through the night and arrived early the next morning as the sun came up. Being accustomed to the sleepy atmosphere of Abu Dhabi I was completely overwhelmed by the cranes, large machines, trucks and oil installations that were all over Das Island. They were building a harbour, a loading terminal and storage tanks as well as expanding facilities for the employees. The infrastructure they had developed there in only a few years was incredible.

In fact, Das Island was so far ahead in modern amenities that comparing it to my home in Abu Dhabi would be like comparing the Abu Dhabi of today with one of the uninhabited islands off its shores. I stayed with my uncle in a room which had an electric lamp and a fan, an experience in modernisation beyond my wildest dreams. Included in the amazing things I saw was an open-air cinema where the audience watched recent English films sitting in chairs instead of in the sand. The whole atmosphere was electric to me, everything was new and seemed so advanced. The houses, although made of prefabricated material, were well insulated and had pitched roofs so the rain ran off instead of leaking onto the inhabitants within. They even had windows, a feature with which our barasti huts would never be equipped. The food in the mess was incredible: even in the labour camp they offered several varieties of fish, meat, rice and vegetables at meal times. There was bread and butter, even marmalade, in the mornings. There were salt and pepper containers on the tables. They had piped water, showers and towels. I had never owned a towel; here there were towels for everyone, an unbelievable luxury. All of these things were unheard of in Abu Dhabi. I was mesmerised, captivated by the modern way of life that was to be enjoyed on Das Island.

I decided then and there that this was the place for me. It was like heaven on earth, so far beyond the reality of my daily life that I could hardly believe that it was not a dream. In a bid to remain in this paradise I asked my uncle if I could stay there with him and work in the canteen. I would have done anything. I was ready to work as a tea boy or a shop helper if it meant that I could continue living in the lap of luxury. But I was only thirteen at the time so my uncle turned me down. By the following week he had decided that if he did not send me back to Abu Dhabi soon I would be corrupted by the fine life I was enjoying - thrice daily showers and food fit for a king!

Before I knew it, I was on my way back home, a "borrowed" towel tucked away with my few belongings as a souvenir of what I had been forced to leave behind. I never asked my uncle if he missed the towel, which became one of my most prized possessions and a reminder of the possibilities that lay beyond the shores of the mainland.

If the visit to Das Island had been like a dream come true, the trip home was without a doubt one of the highlights of my youth. I flew high above the waters and islands of the Gulf in one of the Gulf Aviation Hurons, captivated by the cream-coloured shores and turquoise water below. The return trip took only a fraction of the time it had taken to get there of course. Still, the only other passenger on the plane, a long-time resident of the area, felt we must surely be lost after we had been flying for about an hour. He could not believe that an Englishman, even though he was a pilot, would be able to find his way back to Abu Dhabi without the assistance of someone such as he who knew the waters of the area like the back of his hand. But as he rose and headed to the cockpit to offer his advice, the captain told him to sit down and fasten his seat belt as we would be landing shortly in Abu Dhabi. The trip made a big impression on me. I recounted it constantly to my friends, and anyone else willing to listen, for ages afterwards.

Besides my trip to Das Island, which was of consequence mostly to me, other more important events occurred in 1961 which had far greater significance in terms of their impact on the growth and development of Abu Dhabi.

Two steps forward, one step back
The events of 1961 were driven by the discovery of significant oil

deposits the previous year. In his year end report for 1960 the Dubai Political Agent highlighted the growing importance of oil to Abu Dhabi and the Trucial States when he wrote: "the most significant economic event of 1960 was the published announcement early in the year that Abu Dhabi Marine Areas Ltd. (ADMA) have discovered oil in commercial quantities and have declared their intention to begin production in 1962 from their offshore concession area around Das Island."

While the British kept themselves well informed on the economic developments of the area, particularly those related to their business interests and the oil industry, the local inhabitants were kept in the dark. Their only clues as to what was going on came from rumours circulating in the community, friends or relatives employed by oil companies as manual labourers and their own personal observations. There may not have been much official news but we could see for ourselves that some things were beginning to change.

In February 1961 the sheikhdom's first desalination plant, supplied by a Dubai company and installed a few months earlier, began producing potable water. The plant was set up on the beach near where the cascading volcano fountain now sits on the Corniche. It was a great leap forward for the community. With its commissioning we expected to have an unlimited supply of desalinated water. Unfortunately the quality of the water produced by the desalination plant left much to be desired. The contractor who had sold the Ruler the plant had not provided chlorine to purify the water. It is quite likely that the plant operators did not know they should be adding chlorine after the water was desalinated in order to make it palatable. The result was water that was so heavy that drinking a glassful was like swallowing a cannonball. But it was the only sweet water we had, so we drank it anyway, some people mixing it with a bit of brackish water to take away the heaviness.

While the plant had been projected to produce 14,000 gallons daily from the outset, it had many teething problems. By the time it was fully operational in the autumn of 1961 it was producing 11,000 gallons a day. However, this would have easily met the requirements of our small population if only the proper chemicals had been available. During the several months it took to get the first plant up and running the Ruler ordered a second plant which arrived in August. Unfortunately, the suppliers failed to provide sufficient intake piping to reach the sea and the Ruler neglected to order storage tanks, so the plant stood idle for a long time. In fact I do not recall it ever having produced any fresh water at all.

These halting steps toward progress were terribly frustrating as it always seemed they fell short of meeting our expectations. Either the projects were delayed, or the equipment did not work properly or we lacked the capabilities to operate it. These two desalination plants, one without the proper chemicals and the other without enough pipeline to reach the sea were typical examples of projects gone wrong. There always seemed to be something missing which was a terrible frustration to all concerned.

In addition to the problems with the plants themselves, two other factors dampened our excitement over the new water supply. First, we had to pay for whatever we used – two anna per gallon, a price which was simply out of reach for many of the town's inhabitants. Most, therefore, were forced to continue drinking the brackish water despite the new facility. Secondly, we still faced the task of hauling the water in goat-skin bags or clay urns either by ourselves or with the help of a donkey as few local people had motorised vehicles at the time. Even those who had vehicles had difficulty accessing the one operational plant without getting stuck as it was surrounded by deep soft sand – there was no mud road or even hard-packed track approaching the plant.

Nevertheless, we felt small steps such as the desalination plants were somehow taking us closer to a future which included more modern amenities and a comfortable lifestyle. While the water from the first desalination plant was heavy, we were thankful for it because at least it tasted fresh. Replacing the brackish water we had drunk for centuries with sweet water like that which was available in most of the civilised world at the time was a turning point for us.

During the spring and summer of 1961 the Ruler took an extended trip overseas. While he was away Sheikh Zayed built Abu Dhabi's first mud road. It stretched from the palace to where the Maqta bridge now stands on the way out of town. At the time there was a causeway there which enabled people to cross the channel with either their camels or motorised vehicles. Sheikh Zayed mobilised every available pick-up truck, lorry and any other vehicle in which mud could be transported. Over a period of about three or four months he managed to lay a stretch of mud road about ten feet wide all the way from the edge of the island to the outskirts of the town. It saved people pushing their vehicles across the sand, actually cutting down the time it took to drive outside of Abu Dhabi by almost two hours because people were far less likely to get stuck.

On the educational front, the Ruler asked my father and Khalifa bin Yousef, another prominent businessman from Abu Dhabi, to go to Jordan in search of school teachers to staff the two-year-old school which had been managed until then by a single teacher. As requested, my father and Khalifa bin Yousef flew to Jordan in the autumn where they met with King Hussein. He was kind enough to instruct his

Minister of Education to help them in their task. In spite of the low salary, four hundred rupees monthly, which the Ruler had authorised them to offer potential recruits, they managed to hire about ten teachers. Palestinian and Jordanian educators were in need of employment at the time so they agreed to come to teach in Abu Dhabi for this relatively low wage. With the hiring of this group of teachers the first seeds of Abu Dhabi's Palestinian and Jordanian communities were planted. Prior to their arrival in 1962 we had had little, if anything, to do with these Arab brothers to the north. During the subsequent three decades, however, their presence expanded considerably in Abu Dhabi and they made significant contributions to the growth of our economy.

In the latter part of 1961 Abu Dhabi's increasing importance was formally recognised by the British when Her Majesty's Government's first Political Agent, Colonel J. E. H. Boustead assumed his post on 15 November. Although there had been a political officer stationed in Abu Dhabi from 1955 onwards, he reported to the Dubai based Political Agent who saw to the British interests in all the Trucial States. Additionally, in December, an international telegraph office was finally opened thus facilitating communication with the outside world. Although plans for a telephone system were being prepared, the system itself would not materialise for another two years.

Another factor which had a huge impact on the development of Abu Dhabi throughout the early sixties was the Ruler's decision to impose a ban on any new construction in the town, a ban which lasted until Sheikh Zayed took over in 1966. As a result, there was little infrastructure development before the latter part of the decade. Sheikh Shakhbut believed that development should proceed only on the basis of proper planning. He thought that if construction went ahead without it, new buildings might then have to be demolished thereby causing losses to the owners who might in turn demand compensation from the government. Concerned about the possibility of such negative financial consequences, he decided that no further building whatsoever should be allowed.

This type of decision was characteristic of Sheikh Shakhbut who was very cautious in his dealings and suspicious of any new initiatives that might have hastened the rate of progress in the sheikhdom. In keeping with his guarded attitude toward development he maintained a tight grip on the purse strings and an iron-fisted control on everything that went on in Abu Dhabi. While few businesses were being established, for example, anyone who wanted to start a new venture first had to get permission directly from the Ruler. This could be difficult as he was reluctant to put anything in writing because of his prior experience with British agreements. He was wary of written documents believing they always somehow favoured the parties with whom he was negotiating. I learned of Sheikh Shakbut's disinclination to conclude negotiations when, in the spring of 1961, my father welcomed the Kanoo family of Bahrain to our Abu Dhabi home.

Bahraini visitors

The Kanoos were interested in establishing an Abu Dhabi office to represent the shipping and cargo side of their business. Once here, they found that in order to set up shop they first had to get permission from the Ruler then conclude a written agreement with him. Given the Ruler's reluctance to put his signature to almost anything, their task was challenging. They had to convince him first that it was normal business procedure to open an office; secondly, that their proposal to represent shipping companies and airlines here would benefit Abu Dhabians by linking them to the outside world and thirdly, that he should support them in what they were doing. What I remember most of their two month stay in our house is the constant typing and retyping as they amended and rearranged the agreement time after time in an effort to achieve a set of conditions the Ruler would approve. In the end their persistence paid off. With considerable encouragement from my father, Sheikh Shakhbut finally signed an agreement. The Kanoos, however, had to accept all of his terms and conditions in order to get permission to set up their office in Abu Dhabi.

Throughout the negotiations several members of the Kanoo family stayed in our home. My father provided them with whatever comforts we possessed, minimal though they were at the time. We had no electricity or running water, not to mention indoor plumbing facilities. They slept, alongside the rest of us, inside on the floor in the afternoons and outdoors on the roof of my cousin's clay shelter at night. As they had, for the most part, travelled extensively and been educated in England they were accustomed to far more creature comforts, even in Bahrain, than we had ever dreamed of in Abu Dhabi. Living our simple existence must have been a significant adjustment for them, but the Kanoos accepted our hospitality graciously, adapting themselves to our more basic ways during their stay. Later in the same year they in turn welcomed my father, my brother and I at their home in Bahrain, an experience I shall never forget. The trip was the first step in yet another of my father's many business ventures.

Having already owned several motorised vehicles himself, my father had the foresight to realise that the increasing demand for them in Abu Dhabi would eventually lead to a similar demand for spare parts for maintenance and repairs. He decided to shift his business from retailing dry goods and foodstuffs to importing and selling spare parts for automobiles. So he packed up all his shop contents, mostly textiles and foodstuffs, and sold it lock, stock and barrel for about 7,000 rupees. He used the capital to travel to Bahrain where he intended to purchase a range of automotive parts which he felt would sell in Abu Dhabi. My brother and I were lucky enough to accompany him on this buying trip.

It was my second experience on a Gulf Aviation plane and I was just as thrilled the second time around as I had been the first. We landed in Bahrain, though much more smoothly on the proper tarmac runway than we did in Abu Dhabi on the bumpy stretch of sabkha that served as our airstrip. From the moment we landed we saw many sights to delight our youthful eyes. At the airport itself there was a two-storey terminal building, modern and well-maintained. From there we were ushered into a big American saloon car. It was an unforgettable ride, sitting in the back of such a luxurious vehicle driven on a smooth road – the first paved road we had ever seen.

Paradise found

If I had been impressed with Das Island I was completely overwhelmed by Bahrain. The whole atmosphere was futuristic compared to Abu Dhabi. Of course Bahrain's development had progressed much faster than ours from about 1900 onwards. Prior to the twentieth century they had several busy pearl trading centres and their proximity to Saudi Arabia, Basrah and Kuwait contributed to their faster development. In comparison, the Trucial States, particularly Abu Dhabi, were relatively far flung and had little to offer, so they were neglected. While we had established our first and only non-religious school in 1959, their first school had opened nearly four decades earlier in 1921. By 1927 there were Bahrainis graduating from Beirut's American University. They had hospitals in the 1920s, roads and traffic police as far back as 1930, and even a sports club in 1941. Bahrain began exporting oil in 1932; further modernisation financed by the oil revenues started almost immediately. When we visited in 1961 the place was equipped with lots of amenities including piped water and electricity while in the Sheikhdom of Abu Dhabi there was hardly anything. We lived in the eighteenth century while the rest of the world, even the rest of our neighbours, had advanced into the twentieth. We had nothing to offer visitors, we had nothing to export, we had no importance to the outside world whatsoever. Poverty, illiteracy, poor health, a high rate of mortality all plagued us well into the 1960s. We had nothing but our hopes, our dreams of a better tomorrow and our belief in God.

Visiting Bahrain was like taking a trip to another planet. Everything was modern: roads, highways and high-rise buildings. They even had hotels, one of which we stayed in, with air-conditioned rooms and nice dining areas serviced by proper kitchens. The souk was vast and busy, choc-a-bloc with all kinds of exotic items which we had never seen in the Abu Dhabi market: endless bolts of imported fabrics, intricate jewellery, children's toys, radios, household appliances, foodstuffs and furniture. The port was large enough to accommodate several huge ships and we saw big trucks transporting goods back and forth between the town and the docks. Everything we saw in Bahrain was new and exciting.

One of the highlights of the trip was a visit to the Kanoo family's offices, housed in their own five storey building equipped with all the amenities. They had air-conditioning, desks, sitting rooms, typewriters, secretaries, clerks, in fact, all the equipment and personnel required to run a modern office. We could hardly believe that these same people, accustomed to surroundings which included beautiful offices, cars and homes, had stayed with us for months living our simple lifestyle. They invited us to lunch in the building's penthouse suite which also had a dining area. We took the elevator to get up there, another first for my brother and me. We were mystified by the floating box that ferried people, as if by magic, from one floor to the next. In fact we were so enthralled with the sensation of it rising and falling that we rode up and down until someone finally chased us out.

We also visited the Ruler of Bahrain. He had a magnificent majlis, huge by any standards, where he gave us the warmest of welcomes. He was so gracious and kind we did not even think of refusing his invitation to share a meal, which, as we might have expected, was fabulous. There was both an incredible variety and an astounding amount of food – an endless number of exotic dishes in massive quantities for the few of us who were at the table. We felt like characters in the tales of the Thousand and One Nights, sitting with royalty in this beautifully decorated majlis, glittering chandeliers hanging from the ceiling, the people around us dressed in the finest white abbaya wearing the sashes of the royal Bahraini family, the best food laid out for our dining pleasure: it was like being in a dream. Had we had books or newspapers in which we could have read about such things we scarcely would have believed them possible. Yet there we were experiencing them for ourselves. My brother and I were so in awe we could hardly speak or eat.

Like all good things the trip came to an end much too quickly.

During the comparatively short time we were there my father had purchased the inventory he needed to open the automotive shop – mostly Land Rover parts as they were the vehicles of choice in Abu Dhabi at the time. Once we were home life seemed to have lost all its lustre. Having set foot in Bahrain and seen the wonders there it was difficult for my brother and me to accept the primitive facilities we had at home. We became restless and discontented. We could no longer sleep on the floor without thinking of the comfortable air-conditioned room we had enjoyed in Bahrain. We could no longer bathe in the brackish water without thinking how pleasant it was to shower in the crystal clear water of Bahrain. Everything we did we compared with how much better it was in Bahrain. But all our grousing did little good as things did not change in Abu Dhabi one bit. In fact, it would be at least a decade before we even began to catch up with our more modern neighbours and the rest of the world.

While my brother and I bemoaned our fate, our father was making a success of his new venture in the automotive parts business. He came back with the small inventory of parts he had acquired and opened a small shop. This humble beginning was the foundation of the family's present day business which now includes four hotels, several apartment buildings, rental villas, three car importing companies, an oil field services company, a trading company representing Bosch and Michelin tyres, and a travel agency.

Once he opened the shop my father became ever more aware of the importance of modern transportation. He began concentrating on automobiles as well as automotive parts and services. As his business grew over the next few months he went to the British Bank of the Middle East (BBME), requesting their assistance in developing partnerships with suppliers of automotive parts in Britain. He wanted to deal directly with the manufacturers instead of through middlemen in Bahrain. They told him the best way to achieve his objective would be for him to go to the United Kingdom to visit the manufacturers personally with his proposal. He agreed. Saeed Nasser, the assistant manager of commercial accounts at the BBME, accompanied him to act as translator. When they travelled to England during the summer of 1961, my father experienced life in a European country for the first time. As a result of the trip he decided to import reconditioned Bedford trucks from England to Abu Dhabi. His belief that people would find reconditioned vehicles more affordable than new ones was correct. His first consignment of four trucks was spoken for by the time it reached the shores of Abu Dhabi several months later and he had already placed an order for an additional four. He continued to import the reconditioned army vehicles –

around twelve to fourteen yearly – until 1968. They were used primarily for small jobs so their scope as moneymakers was rather limited. This fact, coupled with the lack of roads and the relatively low incomes of the local inhabitants, served to keep demand at a constant level until the latter part of the decade. He began dealing in new vehicles in 1968 when their importation was made more viable with the increased demand fuelled mostly by the local population's ability to pay higher prices.

Chapter 5

The Threshold of Development

Castles in the sand

1962 was yet another year of slow but steady progress in Abu Dhabi. It was most significant, however, for the fact that the first oil shipment was exported from the sheikhdom during the summer. In his annual review to his superiors, Colonel Hugh Boustead, the British Political Agent in Abu Dhabi, made reference to our debut on the international scene:

"On July 5, 1962, the tanker 'British Signal' left Das Island for Europe, carrying the first consignment of oil ever to be shipped from the state of Abu Dhabi. There was a small crop of articles about Abu Dhabi in the European and Arab press and even an item on Radio Moscow. Abu Dhabi had at last emerged from two thousand years of obscurity to the status of an oil-producing state... The fact that oil is now being produced here and that production is likely to increase considerably in the future, bringing great wealth in its train, has dominated events in Abu Dhabi in 1962."

While the rest of the world took note, the most significant event in our recent history went virtually unnoticed in Abu Dhabi itself, even though it represented the beginning of a new era. It should have been a day for celebration as we looked forward with anticipation to the increased wealth the oil industry would bring and the bright future that lay ahead of us. Instead, it went by unmarked, in Abu Dhabi, another day like any other. Even though a ceremony was held on Das Island I personally remember little about that milestone in the history of Abu Dhabi and I believe few of my compatriots would remember it either, even though it was of major importance to the sheikhdom and its people.

Despite this laudable achievement and the promise of future wealth, Abu Dhabi continued to take only small tentative steps toward development rather than the great strides which would later be made under the leadership of Sheikh Zayed. Throughout 1962, and over the next few years, the British persisted in trying to persuade Sheikh Shakhbut to initiate the much-needed infrastructure improvements that would allow Abu Dhabi to thrive. In an effort to overcome the ban on new construction which had been imposed by Sheikh Shakhbut in 1961, the British Political Agency went all out trying to put together a development plan for the town. Engineers and consultants arrived full of ideas and long-term plans. British firms were contracted to follow through and implement them. Construction would be financed with the revenues the oil companies were projecting for the subsequent five years. Everything was in place. Naturally, as with anything in which the British became involved they stood to gain significantly from the proposals. British companies would do the work and, ultimately, British interests would gain further from the developments they planned. Still, Abu Dhabi would have gained a great deal as well. Sheikh Shakhbut, however, would have none of it. He remained on bad terms with the British authorities, suspicious of anything and everything they suggested. He met with the British Political Agent regularly, listened to his proposals and agreed with him on the spot, but once the Political Agent turned his back the Ruler did nothing to follow through and get the development process rolling.

Of course all of this was frustrating for the British authorities but it was the people of Abu Dhabi who suffered most as a result. Despite the lack of public information, the rumour mill was churning. By the middle of the year everyone knew oil was being exported from Das Island and revenues were being generated as a result. They also knew there had to be money in the bank and yet, up to that point, their lifestyle had not changed for the better. On the contrary, it grew more difficult by the day. The demand for housing, supplies and services continued to increase at faster rates as the oil companies developed wells and produced oil in ever greater quantities. Since the oil companies' needs could not be met in the local market they were forced to turn to Bahrain, Qatar and the United Kingdom to procure goods, services and technical expertise. The people of Abu Dhabi could see them importing cars, trucks, materials and equipment but since nothing was being bought here, there was no benefit to the local economy. The local merchants could not provide the needed products and services nor could they accommodate the increasing number of oil workers because they lacked capital and were forbidden from building anything.

By the middle of the year three banks had established operations in Abu Dhabi town. The British Bank of the Middle East had been first to set up shop. It was followed by the Eastern Bank in 1961 and the Ottoman Bank in early 1962. Even they, however, could not help the local merchants because they did not have the accounting or administrative systems required to handle modern business banking needs. To add to the misery of the locals, especially the merchants, there was no government administration to help them organise themselves to take advantage of the opportunities arising from the growth of the oil industry. The people who might have provided products and services could not do so because they lacked the skills and the infrastructure. Most of them spoke little English, so on top of everything there was a communication gap. The local business community was simply not plugged into the system; it was ill-equipped, both financially and administratively, to take advantage of new opportunities. Neither were local entrepreneurs helped or encouraged by the government to participate in the promising economic growth, slow though it was at the time. The whole situation was extremely frustrating for all concerned.

As a result, Abu Dhabi was being left far behind in the development race. Many of the oil field suppliers were located in Dubai. It grew more important as a commercial centre and benefited significantly from the oil-related activity in Abu Dhabi. The Dubai-based suppliers met the needs of the oil exploration, drilling and onshore operations in Tarif and Jebel Dhanna as well as the offshore facilities at Das Island. Qatar was also thriving as a result of the oil industry in Abu Dhabi. It already had a well-developed oil industry infrastructure which had been up and running for some time. The Qataris were thus able to provide a certain amount of expertise in the area of supplies and oil field services. We were in the sad position of being dwarfed by our neighbours on either side. Unfortunately Abu Dhabi's growth was being stunted by the poor relationship that existed between the Ruler and the British authorities.

Deteriorating relations

As time went on the relationship worsened, soon expanding to encompass anyone - including the oil companies - whom the Ruler felt might be in collusion with the British government. Shortly after the first export of 33,000 tons of oil from Das Island in July 1962 the Ruler and Abu Dhabi Marine Areas (ADMA) began arguing over how, and how much, he would be paid for his share of the oil revenues. ADMA had a signed agreement stating that he should receive twenty per cent of the proceeds of the sale at the accepted market price. The Ruler, however, felt he was entitled to take physical possession of twenty per cent of the oil shipment then set the price at which his share would be sold. They explained to him the virtual impossibility of his plan. He was furious. Despite the fact that he had no oil storage facilities, nor the expertise nor the administrative infrastructure to sell it on the international market, he was insistent that he was being hoodwinked by ADMA. He categorically refused to accept the calculations of the company representatives, believing they were somehow conspiring to cheat him of his rightful share of the profits. This episode further worsened the already poor relationship between the Ruler and Her Majesty's Government. He blamed the British for all the misunderstandings between himself and ADMA as he believed the latter was controlled and owned by the former.

He continued to look for other business partners but was thwarted by the British who controlled the issuing of visas for visitors to the sheikhdom by virtue of their jurisdiction over the foreign affairs of Abu Dhabi. Since they did not wish him to speak with their European and North American competitors they simply refused to issue them visiting visas. Because the Ruler had little contact with the Germans, French and Americans, who were discouraged by the British Political Agent from visiting, he was unable to solicit advice or ideas from any other source but the British whom he deeply mistrusted. The fact that he was backed into a corner might explain his stubborn refusal to co-operate in any way with the British government or its representatives.

Meanwhile, the people of Abu Dhabi continued to live simple, primitive lives. However, the hardships to which we were accustomed were not nearly as easily endured by our foreign visitors. The lack of fresh water, for example, was becoming an acute problem. The two small desalination plants which had been commissioned in 1961 were not sufficient to meet the growing needs of the community. The Ruler made additional efforts to address the water issue in the summer of 1962 when he hired a British engineer and dowser, a Mr. Merrylees, to find water on the island of Abu Dhabi. Merrylees arrived with his diviner's rod in July and began searching for fresh water. He pinpointed various locations in the hopes of finding something better than the brackish water we had been forced to drink as long as anyone could remember. With great fanfare, a drilling rig borrowed from ADMA and much determination on the part of Merrylees, several holes were subsequently drilled in August. Unfortunately none struck fresh water so the holes were capped – not well enough as it turned out as they filled with salt water which then overflowed and flooded part of the town for several months afterward. Though unsuccessful in his bid to find water – despite the promise of a large bonus from the ruler – Merrylees also claimed there was oil beneath the island sands, much to the chagrin of the oil companies. Since he had not heard of this oil before, the Ruler immediately suspected both ADMA and ADPC of withholding information. More fuel was added to the flames of mistrust burning fiercely in Shakhbut's heart.

After the diviner's failure the Ruler finally contracted, in November, to build another small desalination plant, the construction of which was to be completed in the first quarter of the

Leaving for the UK. Well wishers on the air strip 1964. I am 4th from the left.

The First Abu Dhabian students sent to study in England from left to right
Mohammed Al Duhaim; Mohammed Sultan AlYousif; Harib B. Bendoug; Saeed
Omran; Yousef Ameri; Mohammed Darwish Karam; the Author; Hamsa Ameri;
Abdullah Al-Fahim; Jumaa Muhairi.

The banquet that never was. Waiting, (I am third from right), with my father, for the pig to appear

Schooldays - My brother and I about to take the train to Weston Super Mare. 1964

Abu Dhabi girl collecting drinking water. 1963

With my British guardian Mr. Brian Jackson.
General view of Abu Dhabi from ADMA offices. 1962

The Souk-Abu Dhabi town. 1962

Travelling on camel back was the only
form of transport before 1960

(above left) With the introduction of cars in 1961 petrol had to be brought to Abu Dhabi in steel drums.

(above right) Abu Dhabi's first airport, 1961.

A Gulf Aviation (DC3) on Abu Dhabi's air strip. 1961

Bedouin encampment in the desert.

The women of Abu Dhabi
selling fish and produce
in the souk 1961

The Rulers Palace,
The Old Fort, dominates
the Abu Dhabi skyline. 1961

The Eid prayer after Ramadan 1962.

As children we wanted to emulate Sheikh Zayed.

(Left) At an official gathering, from left: Col. J.E.H Boustead, Political Agent;
Saleem Ali Moosa (Agency Interpreter); Sheikh Shakhbut Bin Sultan (Ruler);
Mohammed B. Khalifa Al-Nahyan; Sheikh Zayed Al-Nahyan
(Ruler of Eastern Province).

(above) Tracks in the sand approaing Abu Dhabi town. 1954

(left) Desalinated water still had to be poured into cans and loaded o donkeys for the journey home 196

(top right) Abu Dhabi sea shore a main centre of activity. 1960

(opposite) The sea shore, now the Corniche, Today.

(above) My father, centre, with his next door neighbours Sheikh Tahnoon - left - and Sheikh Mubarak - right -.1994
(top right) Fishermen mending their nets.

(opposite) Our Dubai dream project "The Holiday Centre" complex.

110   A friendship that spans more than 50 years, My father, left, with Sheikh Zayed.

Below; The town of
Abu Dhabi with its
barasti houses and first
main road. 1961

With, from left, my father
and my uncles Ahmed and
Abdul Rahim and my brot
Abdulla. 1993

following year.

In the meantime, construction of the town's first real hotel was finished toward the end of the summer. The "Abu Dhabi Beach Hotel," as it was called, was built by the Bustanis of Lebanon who own the Construction and Trading Company of Beirut (called the CAT Company). The twenty-five room hotel, located near where the Sheraton Hotel stands now, was considered a significant achievement of which Abu Dhabians were very proud. It even had electricity provided by a generator. We sometimes drove there with our father but their prices were way beyond our reach. A soft drink at the hotel cost three rupees - four times the price we paid for a drink at the souk. While we told all our visitors about the facility, the local people were rarely seen frequenting the hotel, in part because of the high prices, but also because it was a considerable distance from the town. A four-wheel drive vehicle was required to get there, making it less accessible to the locals, many of whom still did not have motorised transportation. So the hotel was used primarily by oil company representatives and other visitors.

Needless loss

While they were important to all Abu Dhabians, the milestones of 1962 were insignificant for my family when compared with the tragic death of my mother in the spring of that year. She was seven months pregnant when she went into premature labour. There were still no doctors, nurses or other trained medical practitioners residing in Abu Dhabi so there was no one to attend her other than a local mid-wife whose skills were not sufficient to save my mother from the complications associated with the early labour. Both my mother and her baby died during the delivery. She was only thirty.

Whenever I remember her death I am still angered by the fact that we had no proper medical facilities in Abu Dhabi at the time. Most people around the world, and even here in the Gulf region, were enjoying the best in medical services, yet we did not have a nurse, let alone a doctor, in Abu Dhabi. This was 1962, not the dark ages. Either our government or the British could have easily afforded to provide medical care but nobody wanted to be responsible for the cost. So instead of benefiting from proper health care, our lives were made more difficult. People died from treatable diseases and fever because those who had the power to change things were either unwilling or too mean to do so.

At the time of my mother's death, I had four brothers and sisters: the eldest was fifteen, the youngest was seven. All five of us were left without our primary care-giver to raise us. It was a devastating loss. When she was alive, our whole family - my father, mother, brothers and sisters - all lived under one roof. But when she died, my siblings and I were separated to be cared for by our aunts, cousins and other relatives. We lived in the same compound but we no longer lived in the same house, as we had when my mother was alive. Of course we still had our father; when he was gone our extended family loved and cared for us as best they could. But our relatives had their own children to look after so we often had to fend for ourselves. At meal times we ate with our extended family, all of us from the same plate in the Arab tradition. But even though we were still small we washed our own clothes, dressed ourselves and even bought our own new clothing from the souk during the Eid. In those days we did not buy what we wanted any time we liked, we waited until the Eid, either at the end of Ramadan or during the Haj, which is the traditional time to buy new garments.

Being young at the time we did not fully comprehend the loss we had suffered with the death of our mother. As we grew older we came to know that we had missed an important part of our upbringing as well as a guiding light at a time when darkness prevailed all around us. I suppose we were lucky to have a big family with lots of uncles, aunts and cousins who rallied around us, each trying to provide us with whatever he or she could; and, had it not been for God's providence, guidance and wisdom, we might have suffered far more than we did. As always in life, as well as in death, we must simply accept the will of God. It is through acceptance that my family and I overcame the tragic loss of my mother, suffered so many years ago.

The Arab voice

In the following year, 1963, we again took a few more small steps forward in the painfully slow march of progress.

There were three major developments in the area of communications: the opening of the first post office, an increase in the number of battery-operated radios and the installation of a telephone system.

Sheikh Shakhbut inaugurated the town's first post office in March thus speeding up the mail service between Abu Dhabi and the rest of the world. Previously, all letters had been delivered by hand so there had not been much correspondence, people simply did not write to each other unless they had to. The postal authority promised to reduce the two-week delivery time for ordinary mail travelling from London to Abu Dhabi to only three days.

The second, and perhaps the most important in terms of the economic well-being of the people here, was the increase in the number of radios in Abu Dhabi, most of them battery operated because we still had no electricity at the time. People began to listen to Radio Cairo, the voice of the Arab world. As they listened they started to realise there was a world beyond the shores of Abu Dhabi, a world full of countries more advanced than ours. They became more informed about what was happening in the Arab world and the Arab League of Nations. They heard the news and the commentaries, following with interest the events which were taking place across the Middle East as a whole.

When the Egyptian broadcasters realised they had an audience in the Gulf, an audience that was living in conditions that would be considered backward by most standards of the times, they directed a certain amount of their commentary to this area. They carried news of events that were either happening here or that might have an impact on us. The people of Abu Dhabi were elated that someone had taken notice of them. The coverage on Radio Cairo sent them an important message, a message that told them they were not as forgotten as they had thought. With this awareness came a greater sense of power and importance, a feeling that they, the people, had something to offer, especially now that there was oil flowing from their land. They learned that the oil could be their ticket to progress and wealth. Because it was important enough to attract the interest of nations from around the world, they felt it would also mean these nations would want to participate in the development of the area.

They began to ask themselves why they had thus far been given less than they deserved. Partly as a result of the radio coverage, as well as other events which were taking place in the rest of the Arab world, some of the local oil workers in the Sheikhdom of Abu Dhabi went on strike in the late spring of 1963. In comparing their scale of pay with that of workers elsewhere, Abu Dhabians employed with the oil companies found their remuneration to be below standard. There were work stoppages in Jebel Dhanna, Tarif and Das Island as local workers demanded better pay and working conditions. Although they were small in number - only about one hundred strong at Jebel Dhanna for example - they insisted their demands be met. The strikes, although short, were intense. The workers succeeded in getting their employers' attention and making them understand they could no longer take the local workforce for granted. As a result, salaries were equalised for offshore and onshore workers, as well as the employees of different contractors; living conditions for all workers were also improved.

The last in the trio of communications developments was the installation of a telephone system in Abu Dhabi town. The British-backed company on the project, International Aeradio Ltd. (IAL), had been established two years earlier, but because of a dispute with the Ruler the system's installation had been delayed until the summer of 1963. The system comprised about seventy telephones in all, most of which were located in the head offices of the oil companies, the British Political Agency and other locations where such devices were needed.

A few days after the telephone system was inaugurated at the beginning of August, a third desalination plant was commissioned in Abu Dhabi. The Ruler contracted with a Kuwaiti company to build a plant capable of producing 25,000 gallons of desalinated water per day, although, like everything else it took time before it ran properly and reached its output capacity. Nevertheless, it was something we appreciated despite the fact that we had to pay a rupee for every thirty-two gallons of water we purchased – this was still less than half the price charged by the other operating desalination plant.

Meanwhile, foreign consultants and contractors continued to make various development proposals to the Ruler. He remained, for the most part, either unconvinced or unwilling to proceed with many improvements. He steadfastly refused, for example, any proposal to generate electricity for the populace of Abu Dhabi town despite the fact that the palace had been electrified by portable generator from about 1961 onwards. However, if the truth be told, it had taken several months of ardent lobbying to convince him to light even the palace. Before proceeding he had to ascertain whether electricity in the palace was a good and useful thing, or whether it was an evil and dangerous thing. He had been told that if one touched a live wire one could be electrocuted and die. The Ruler, concerned for his family's safety and wary of the dangers of an Englishman's invention, was not easily persuaded that the electrification would not pose an undue threat to his loved ones. Once he believed there was no chance of people coming into contact with live wires he agreed to install electricity in his residence. Soon after the decision was made the twenty-year-old palace was lit up like Disneyland. Light shone on the domes as well as the perimeter, it was like a picture book castle in a magic kingdom. We had thought at the time that these bright lights were an indication of what was soon to follow for the rest of the town, but two years later we still found ourselves without electricity and only a little further down the road to progress.

While the Ruler turned down many proposals, he did enter into an agreement with a German company, represented here by a Lebanese businessman Mr Victor Hashim, to proceed with an ambitious two-phased plan to undertake a water resources survey and construct a fully-equipped hospital, two schools, various accommodation complexes, and a police station among other things.

Most of the structures were to be prefabricated, a fact I remember quite clearly from personal experience.

Few amusements

Youngsters growing up in Abu Dhabi had to be very imaginative in finding things to pass the time. We did not play any sports to speak of. We had no facilities and no one to teach us how to play the games such as football which would later become so popular. Consequently our first school sports day, witnessed by the Ruler and all the local inhabitants, consisted of contests requiring little equipment. The event was held next to the grand mosque on a flat patch of ground where all the youngsters competed enthusiastically in running, jumping and tug-of-war. Because we had no organised extra-curricular activities, we kept ourselves occupied after school playing marbles, jacks or spinning tops – made with a wooden peg, a nail, and a piece of string – on the sabkha or in the souk. On Fridays and holidays we spent most of the day either swimming or playing on the beach. In the late afternoon we would play hide-and-seek until dusk turned into the dark of night and we could no longer see where to run or hide. If the evening was moonlit we would play on, although we often sustained injuries from running in the dark barefoot. Aside from school, the sea and our simple games, there were few other amusements.

I was more fortunate than most – I had been given a bicycle by my uncle when I was about fourteen. Three or four of my friends had managed to scrape up enough money to make similar purchases and we rode our bikes together in the souk. It was the only place, other than the distant airstrip, with a surface hard enough for cycling. The shopkeepers sprayed water on the sand pathway so people could walk in between the shops more easily. This also made the pathways perfect for bike riding. The shopkeepers, however, did not always share our enthusiasm for the sport as we careered around the souk with gay abandon. The alley between the shops was not much more than a meter wide and it became congested with customers, especially on Thursday and Friday afternoons. When they reached the limit of their patience the shopkeepers would chase us out. In that case we had to find a small area of dry sabkha where we could ride, mostly around and around in circles. Sometime after the Ruler contracted to build the town's first hospital, however, we had a new place to play our cycling games.

The prefabricated materials, packed in huge boxes, were delivered to a site about two kilometres from the town centre where the ground was relatively hard. The site became our new playground. We would push our bicycles across the sand so we could ride freely, playing hide and seek amongst the huge boxes containing the future hospital. Whenever we had a school holiday or even when we felt there was nothing worthwhile to learn, we would take the day off, escape to our favourite spot and cycle or picnic in the shade of the boxes. Even today when I drive by the Central Hospital I think of the place where I spent many pleasurable hours cycling or picnicking.

Fortunately for us, but unfortunately for the sick and ill of Abu Dhabi, the project was derailed and the prefabricated hospital sat there in boxes for more than two years. While it was great fun for us to spend our leisure hours in their shadows, the fact that the boxes of material lay there for so long was sad for the people of the community. It meant they were still not getting the kind of medical care they should have at the time. The hospital lay there for so long because of a misunderstanding between Sheikh Shakhbut and the suppliers of the prefabricated structure. He believed they would supply the materials for the hospital and erect it as well. The contractors, on the other hand, felt their contract had been fulfilled once they delivered the materials to the site. In any case, the future hospital sat there in pieces for a very long time, until somebody finally got the project rolling. Abu Dhabi's first hospital, the Central Hospital, was later opened in 1966.

Apart from those boxes my last childhood memories of the early 1960s are of the simple lives we lived then – even the souk was small and uninspiring. In those days it consisted of two rows of shops, about thirty of them in total, that faced each other across an alley. Some of the shops had mud walls capped with roofs of mud and palm fronds while others were made of palm fronds only. Each of them was about nine square metres. Most sold more or less the same goods, usually dried food stuffs such as rice, flour, sugar and coffee as well as textiles. There were no ready made garments for sale then; cloth was bought at the souk then taken either to the tailor or back home to be stitched by hand. Before 1960 the shops had little merchandise that might be of interest to children. No toys, no sweets, no biscuits, nothing that a child with a coin in his or her pocket could buy. By 1963 some of the shopkeepers had brought in sweets, dried biscuits, even dried powdered orange juice and marbles for our games. Some started serving lemonade in bottles! That was when we began to realise the value and the power of money. The possibility of actually being able to buy something as delightful as lemonade with our coins opened a whole new world for us.

Once we began coveting the prizes in the souk we worked very hard to either earn or wheedle a coin or two from our relatives. I remember asking my father for some money one day as he left for Al

Ain on one of his many trips. He reached in his pocket to draw out a single rupee, telling me it was the last one he had. But he gave it to me all the same. I have never forgotten his generosity that day because it meant he would be travelling between Abu Dhabi and Al Ain with no cash in his pocket. Not that there was much to spend money on during that trip at the time - there was nothing but sand dunes and the occasional bedouin encampment along the way. Nevertheless, whenever I remember my father giving me that single rupee, I think of the vast differences between our lives then and now.

Despite the huge changes, however, some of the traditions of my childhood live on and are practised today by my own young children. Youngsters today are still given gifts at Eid just as we were then. We were also given token gifts or money during the Eids, either at the end of Ramadan or during the Haj period. We went from house to house as some children do at Halloween to gather either sweets and chocolates, or coins. Sometimes we were given canned milk, brought over from Das Island, or what they called sherbet, a powdered orange juice that was diluted with water. Other than at the Eids, the only time we had sweets was when one of our relatives or friends came back on leave from Das Island or Tarif bringing with them a box of chocolates or a container of sweets from the camp. Apart from that we had few treats. Because sweets were relatively scarce people often gave us money at the Eid when they could spare it. If we were lucky they would give us a fraction of a rupee. After three days of visiting the neighbours' houses we might end up with five rupees in our pocket - a considerable fortune which we would quickly squander by buying whatever candies and trinkets caught our fancy from the few that were available in the souk. We often spent all our money in less than a day. But this did not worry us in the least as we had nowhere to keep coins anyway! Our kandouras were not fitted with pockets until much later in the decade because we never had anything to put in them until then.

Cinema and secrets

We were very fortunate indeed to have one form of evening entertainment - the ADMA beach-side cinema. Once or twice a week the oil company was kind enough to show films, just as Sheikh Zayed had done at his palace in Al Ain. I remember them bringing a 16mm projector, installing it on a wooden platform out in the open air near the beach then showing a film using a white-washed wall of a house as a screen. Everybody sat in the sand and watched. They showed many English films. We did not understand the words or the stories but we watched them anyway as we had little else to do. Once in a while they ran a western film, the ultimate in action entertainment as far as we were concerned. We loved to see the cowboys in their strange hats, riding horses and firing from their six-shooters. Sometimes, much to our delight and amazement, they would show a cartoon before the film started. We were captivated by the animated characters and their crazy antics. We never accepted that our favourites, Tom and Jerry and Mickey Mouse, were mere drawings, the result of some faraway cartoonist's vivid imagination. We believed them to be real characters acting their parts just as the people did in the films that followed. No one could convince us that they were just drawings on paper and film, we were such loyal and devoted fans.

Needless to say, the oil companies were doing a lot more at the time than showing films. It seemed that only a privileged few people, however, were actually aware of the scope and the details of their activities in Abu Dhabi. Unbeknown to most Abu Dhabians, including us young cinema-goers, the sheikhdom achieved a second major milestone in the escalating growth of its oil industry late in 1963. On 14 December, the tanker Esso Dublin left from the Jebel Dhanna terminal some 250 kilometres west of Abu Dhabi town. The 33,818 tons of crude oil on board were the first to be shipped from the mainland Abu Dhabi oil field at Bab. Despite the significance of the event for this tiny piece of desert, its inhabitants and, in fact, for the rest of the world, the momentous day passed without fanfare and little more than a whisper of the news amongst the local people. There were articles in the British press which projected the 1964 and 1965 royalty income from the oil exports at £10 million and £25 million respectively, but no official word came from the palace to tell us of the milestone or what it would eventually mean to our modest lives. Even when the terminal was officially inaugurated in March of the following year only Sheikh Shakhbut and a few of his followers were invited to attend. It appeared no one wanted the local people to participate in the success story of the oil industry other than by providing their labour at cheap rates. In spite of the veil of secrecy that seemed to cloak everything associated with the oil activities, we heard rumours of the incredible revenues that were being generated. We began to look forward to the development we felt must be imminent.

Sadly, it would still be a long time before we saw any of the wealth that came from the exploitation of our oil resources. Our lifestyle stayed as it had been - primitive and simple - until 1966 when Sheikh Zayed took over the rulership of Abu Dhabi. Only then did our lives change significantly as a result of the oil revenues that had been accumulating in the coffers for over a decade.

While some major milestones were being achieved in the

sheikhdom, albeit quietly, during 1963, it was also an important year for me personally. With the increase of foreigners coming to Abu Dhabi, particularly white collar workers, demand for housing, transportation and other services was on the rise. My father saw an opportunity to expand his business in automotive services by becoming more deeply involved in the importation and sale of automobiles rather than just second hand army trucks. He decided to explore the possibility of becoming the exclusive Abu Dhabi agent for one or more major car manufacturers. Over the previous several years he had befriended a number of visitors to Abu Dhabi, foreign businessmen from Lebanon, England, Germany and Denmark whom he thought might be able to help him make contact with the appropriate people within the automobile industry. He planned a spring business trip. Several days before he was due to leave he asked me if I had a passport, which I did thanks to our trip to Bahrain the previous year. He then told me that I, along with his Indian secretary, would be joining him on his business trip to Lebanon and Europe.

Faraway places

We set off a few days later, flying first to Bahrain and then on to Beirut. I was flabbergasted by Beirut. I had never seen such mountains and greenery and the weather was fabulous. It had been hot in Abu Dhabi when we left but the air in Beirut was cool, clear and refreshing. The hustle and bustle of this vibrant city with its beautiful hotels and historic buildings took my breath away. We stayed for a few days before flying to Germany, a country of clean and modern cities full of glass towers the likes of which I had never seen before. We visited the Mercedes company and its museum where I was astonished to discover that cars had been manufactured long before the first vehicle arrived in Abu Dhabi! Little did I know that this brief introduction to antique cars would develop into a much loved hobby many years later. While I drank in the sights and sounds of Germany my father focused on his business negotiations. Things went well with the company. While we were there he signed an agreement naming him as the first and only Mercedes distributor in Abu Dhabi.

Once my father's business was complete in Germany we went on to Denmark which was also very beautiful. But it was our last stop that was the pinnacle of the trip for me.

Naturally I had heard of London before, on the radio and from the British who were in Abu Dhabi. I knew it would be something special. Nevertheless I was ill-prepared, in more ways than one, for the reality of the city itself. It surpassed even my wildest expectations, but I was so travel weary during our stay that I only experienced a fraction of what I might have during that first visit. With the change in climate and the constant fog and smog that enveloped the city I lost complete track of time. I was in a daze. My father rose early in the morning, around 4:30 or 5:00 a.m.; he in turn woke me when he felt I had slept long enough, usually at about 6:00 a.m. By the stroke of 8:00 we had eaten our breakfast, left the hotel and were on our way by taxi to one appointment or another. More often than not, however, I was fast asleep again within minutes of getting into the car so exhausted was I from the hectic schedule and the lack of sleep. Of the eleven days of our visit I was probably awake for only half! Whenever cognisant, though, I was completely overwhelmed by the city, gaping in amazement at everything I saw. I was equally enthralled with the many new things I experienced including a short train trip outside the city.

Wherever we travelled, Lebanon, Germany, Denmark, and the UK, we were warmly welcomed by the people we visited. Our hosts invariably showed us the sights and were very kind no matter where we were. On one or two occasions, however, the well-intentioned hospitality yielded unexpected results. One such situation occurred when we were in England.

We were invited to various luncheons and dinners hosted by company representatives with whom we wished to do business. One of them went to a great deal of trouble orchestrating what he had told us would be the culinary highlight of our trip abroad. He went to great lengths to keep the meal fare a secret but tantalised us for days with comments of how splendid it would be. Having told us that he had personally instructed the chef as to the proper preparation of the dish, he assured us we would never have tasted anything like it. On the day of the promised feast the three of us skipped lunch. Our host insisted we must be ravenous at dinner so as not to waste even the tiniest morsel of the delicacy we were to be served. We arrived at his club at 8:00 p.m. sharp and were seated in one of the private dining rooms. We chatted amiably as we waited for the meal to begin. He still refused to reveal the secret of the menu, he wanted it to be a complete surprise. He did mention though, that it had taken several days to prepare the main course which had to be marinated before being cooked to his exact specifications. By this time we were almost as curious as we were hungry. Finally it arrived, a huge rack of smoked meat on a massive silver platter. It certainly looked appetising. As it turned out, however, our host had been right about only one thing, we had most definitely never tasted anything like it. Nor would we that night. We were embarrassed to find, as we sat with the feast before us, that the meat was...pork. Just as some of the ways of the West were still foreign to us, so was the unfortunate company representative ignorant of the dictates of Islam.

Another surprise awaited us in Paris where we were picked up at the airport by a taxi driven by a blond woman. Our jaws dropped in shock. We had never seen a woman driving before, yet here was one behind the wheel. Not only did she drive but she had golden hair the colour of the Abu Dhabi sands! Unfortunately our lack of French and her lack of Arabic prevented us from ever finding out how she had come to be a taxi driver, but having her as our chauffeur was an experience we would never forget.

All of these adventures, even those which were a little uncomfortable, were exciting. So much so that when we finally returned home all I could do was think about going back to Europe, especially to England. I wanted to live there. I wanted to start a new life there. I could not accept the fact that there was such a vast difference between the countries I had seen and visited and the place that was my home. We still did not have electricity in Abu Dhabi. No roads. No indoor plumbing. No modern appliances. We walked everywhere, barefoot through the deep sand. Before I saw Europe I had no idea there were countries where there was no sand at all. I was amazed. I had thought everyone lived as we did, in the desert surrounded by sand, but apparently it was not so.

Even after my trips to Das Island and Bahrain, which overwhelmed me at the time, I did not realise there were more things to experience than life as we lived it in Abu Dhabi and the Arabian Gulf. I had no idea of the infinite possibilities until I saw them during that first European trip, it was an unforgettable eye-opener. Everything I saw I was seeing for the first time, like a new baby discovering the world around him. When I got home it was hard for me to convey the wonder of what I had seen to my friends and family. How could I explain to them that there was a park, called Hyde Park, in the middle of London, which was bigger than Abu Dhabi town? They had never seen grass, other than desert scrub, or trees other than date palms and hardy desert bushes. How could I explain the Thames, a huge fresh-water river, when they had never seen a natural stream that flowed all year round? How could I describe the tall buildings when the highest structure we had was the Ruler's palace? It was unimaginable.

I felt fortunate to have been taken to these faraway countries and to have seen the things I had, although I was too young at the time to understand why we did not have the same in Abu Dhabi. As a people we were thankful for each step toward modernisation no matter how small it was. A desalination plant, a post office, a mud road, these were significant achievements in the long march of progress. Like most Abu Dhabians, I did not know we were so far behind the rest of the world. I did not understand that we lacked education, I thought by reading the Quran we knew everything we needed to know. After my visit abroad I still knew the Quran to be the foundation for everything, but I also understood there were even more things to learn than the lessons of the Holy Book. When I returned to school the other students would sometimes turn to me as somewhat of an expert on the life beyond our shores. Of course I was still very naive, not nearly as worldly as I liked to think, but I was one of the very few local children who had ventured so far afield.

I astonished my friends with stories of what I had seen and experienced - electricity that lit up a room with the mere flick of a switch, saloon cars that did not get stuck in the middle of town, double-decker buses, twenty-two storey glass buildings, underground trains ferrying hundreds of people from one end of a huge city to another, ships the size of islands the likes of which we had never seen in our waters, cool weather in the summer - so cool in fact that we had to dress up to keep warm! Most captivating of all was television, an amazing invention that brought the faces of strangers and movie-like images into one's hotel room. As I told the stories they sometimes sounded unreal even to me who had been there and seen it all with my own eyes. Here we were in Abu Dhabi, still, literally, in the dark, living in huts which, even if we had power, could not have been wired to provide electricity, the most simple of the wonders I had experienced.

In addition to having been introduced to countless marvels, I also began to learn English, a language which fascinated me the moment I first heard it spoken. Although there were a growing number of British citizens in Abu Dhabi at the time I had little exposure to English before our 1963 trip. However, I picked up the odd word associated with the social graces, "Please", "Thank you", and the like, during our stay in the U.K. I was much impressed with this foreign language and became determined to learn as much as I could in anticipation of my return to England. I dreamed I would return there some day, if not to live then perhaps to go to school. I might as well have been thinking of travelling to the moon, or so I thought at the time.

A dream come true

By the first quarter of 1964 there was a lot of expectation in the air and hopeful signs that things would be changing drastically in Abu Dhabi. The first oil revenue payments - a percentage of the profits generated as a result of the first oil exports - had actually been paid and amounted to over four million pounds. It was only natural that some of this income should find its way into the system and down the channels to the inhabitants in one way or another. A few local people began to benefit in small ways from the oil revenues, although the benefits to the inhabitants were in no way commensurate with the vast wealth that was being created.

Nevertheless, people remained hopeful that massive change was just around the corner. With this belief came the realisation that they were poorly equipped to deal with what was to come. Few could read or write and there was no way of learning the new ways, new languages or new administrative skills they would need to contribute as well as take advantage of the growth that was bound to occur eventually. They looked to their children to carry them into the future. They began to understand the importance of education and to deplore the fact that there was no proper schooling for the next generation in Abu Dhabi. Sadly, their elder children had already missed the chance of an education when they were young. Now that many held menial jobs with the oil companies, either onshore or offshore, it was difficult for them to return to school because their families could not manage without the income they earned. It was a frustrating dilemma. People sensed what was happening but there was little they could do to change the situation.

My father and my family were more fortunate than most as the importance of education had been instilled in them by my grandfather. At the beginning of the year the British Political Agent in Abu Dhabi was exploring the possibility of sending some of the younger boys from here to the UK to study English over the summer. The person he contacted, a Mr Brian Jackson from Maidenhead in England, was so interested when he heard about the project that he decided to come to Abu Dhabi and see the place for himself.

He arrived sometime in February or March. During his visit he interviewed prospective students. My name, as well as my brother Abdullah's, had been forwarded to him. When he came to Abu Dhabi he stopped by my father's shop to meet us. However, talking about the possibility of sending a child to England to study was quite different from actually being able to afford to do so. My father expressed both a willingness and a desire to send both of us but he could not afford all the expenses which included return flights, school fees, pocket money and so forth. He said he would think about it and inform Mr Jackson of his decision later. As it happened, Sheikh Zayed was in Abu Dhabi at the time and my father told him about his quandary. Sheikh Zayed immediately offered to pay for the airline tickets if my father paid for the school fees and other expenses. The British Political Agent agreed to make the necessary arrangements. It was the cooperation of these three parties – our father, Sheikh Zayed and the British Political Agent – that enabled us to take advantage of this fantastic opportunity. That is how my brother and I, aged fifteen and sixteen respectively, came to set off for England in the spring of 1964. We left Abu Dhabi, from the flat sabkha area that still served as the town's airport, on one of the weekly Gulf Aviation flights to Bahrain, then we travelled on to England via Beirut.

The trip was uneventful. Mr Jackson met us at Heathrow airport, then put us on a train to Weston-super-Mare in Somerset where we stayed for the summer with a lovely family who had children our age. Of course everything was new to us. Other than my first short visit to London two years earlier, I had had very little contact with foreign families and the British way of life; my brother had even less. We had to learn almost everything from scratch. First, for example, how to eat with a knife and fork, then how to appreciate fully the different types of food we were offered. The family we stayed with was kind and understanding and took very good care of us. They began teaching us the basic customs of Western culture - how to eat, dress, speak and read - thereby preparing us for the schools we were to attend in September. Despite their kindness and best efforts, however, both my brother and I were terribly homesick. Having dreamed of travelling to England to go to school, we soon found the reality somewhat less magical than the stuff of our fantasies. We missed our father, our brothers and sisters, our cousins, and our aunts and uncles. We wanted desperately to go back to Abu Dhabi. The three months that we had been away already seemed like an eternity to us, separated as we were from our family for the first time in our lives.

But my father insisted, in his letters, that we should stay at least until the autumn to try a proper school. He advised Mr Jackson who then made arrangements for me to go to a school in Lincolnshire while my brother was sent to Westgate-on-Sea in Kent. It was a novel experience for both of us. We learned how to behave like our fellow students, studied hard and soon began to grow accustomed to our new life. As it turned out it was a great experience and we had a lot of fun. We were not as homesick as we had been during the first three months. Of course life became more interesting as we learned new things and began enjoying the company of our fellow students.

Still, when the Christmas holidays arrived we could not resist the temptation of going home, even though we knew it might mean never coming back to England because of the high cost of travelling to and fro. We flew back via Rome, Beirut and Bahrain before once again landing on the sabkha airstrip in Abu Dhabi.

Dust in the wind

Having left Abu Dhabi at a time when the expectation of change seemed at a peak, we fully believed the town, if not the entire sheikhdom, would have been transformed in our absence. Our own expectations had grown unchecked, particularly since there was no telephone service between England and Abu Dhabi. We exchanged letters with our family, though relatively infrequently, so there was no one to tell us that our hopes were like dust in the wind. There were hints in the correspondence, inferences that nothing had changed but we felt in our hearts that there must be some kind of mistake. How could my brother and I be living in such a modern society when our family and friends lived in the dark ages back home? Our people must have gone beyond living in huts, walking barefoot in the sand and hauling their water in goat skins. We refused to believe that when we returned, we would find everything as it had been when we left six months earlier. Surely, we said to ourselves, some progress had been made....

In our dreams we fervently hoped to find Abu Dhabi reborn like a butterfly, a beautiful shining city freed from its dusty desert cocoon. But our own expectations were way out of line with the reality of what had happened, or rather, with what had *not* happened during our absence. Even the final leg of the trip home was an indication of the many obstacles that still had to be overcome on the road to progress.

I was travelling alone as my brother Abdullah had left England before me. I made what I thought would be my last transit stop in Bahrain, only to discover there was no onward flight to Abu Dhabi because the sabkha runway was flooded with rainwater that had fallen throughout the month. No landings were possible until the strip was either pumped dry or dried on its own. I waited a week in Bahrain during which I was in constant contact with Gulf Aviation. They finally suggested that I take an oil company charter to Tarif where I could be picked up and driven to Abu Dhabi. The oil company graciously agreed to let me have a seat on one of its charter flights.

I was met in Tarif by a friend, Sulaiman Khansaheb, whose father was responsible for building the first causeway between Abu Dhabi island and the mainland in 1952. He was in Tarif working for his father's company which was a sub-contractor for the oil company based in Tarif and drilling in Habshan. He drove me to the causeway at Maqta in his Land Rover where I was greeted by my father and my brother who had brought me a wonderful gift: my first car. It was a used 1964 sky-blue Chevrolet saloon car equipped, of course, with the requisite balloon tyres for driving in Abu Dhabi. I was thrilled with the gift which I drove proudly into town on the mud road built by order of Sheikh Zayed in 1961. However, my delight with the car soon turned to disappointment when I found that nothing at all had changed at home. Everything was exactly as I had left it. There was still no electricity and people continued to live in palm-frond huts. From reading the articles in the British newspapers about the incredible income and the oil wealth of Abu Dhabi I felt sure the place would have been transformed. I was heartbroken to discover it was not.

Once back in Abu Dhabi I was a little like a fish out of water. Returning to the local school was out of the question – I had already learned more during my six months in England than my former classmates would glean in the next two years. Besides, the local school still lacked the proper equipment, qualified teachers and an atmosphere that was conducive to learning. Instead of going back there I began helping my father in the spare parts shop trying to gain some insight into the world of business. I caught on quickly. When my father decided to open a branch in Al Ain I worked with the manager Mr Ahmed bin Hamel and played a part in setting it up. But after a few months my father told me that it would better for me to go back to England to further my education – a decision that proved to be of enormous benefit to me in the years to come.

I returned to Lincolnshire for the spring term in 1965 to continue at the school there. After graduating in 1966, I worked as an apprentice at the Ottoman Bank in London for nine months. During that time I was given the responsibility, jointly with Mr Brian Jackson who was still my guardian, of looking after several other young Abu Dhabi boys who were doing as my brother Abdullah and I had done by coming to England to study. By the time I left the country the following year, an office had been established in London to take over the supervision of the students whose numbers increased exponentially over the years until they reached the thousands in the 1990s. In helping the boys I had the opportunity to repay, at least in part, the debt of gratitude I owed to Sheikh Zayed for his efforts in supporting my own education abroad.

I flew back to Abu Dhabi in the autumn of 1967, having not returned here for so much as a visit during the two years I had been away. But this time when I landed, the transformation my compatriots and I had dreamed of for so many years was finally beginning to occur.

Chapter 6

Leaps and Bounds

A charismatic leader

While I was away in England, the event which was to drive the modernisation of Abu Dhabi, so long awaited by all of us, took place – the leadership of the sheikhdom transferred to Sheikh Zayed on 6 August 1966.

My brother and I had seen Sheikh Zayed earlier in the year when he had come to England with my father. They had stayed in a country house about an hour out of London where we had visited them on the weekends. Sheikh Zayed was later followed by two of Sheikh Shakhbut's sons, Sheikh Saeed and Sheikh Sultan, both of whom were in their forties at the time. They stayed in London where we also visited them quite frequently. We had known them both for a long time so they treated us as they would have their own children. They offered us warm hospitality during our short stays and gave us gifts when we returned to school. On one such weekend visit, in the middle of August, I was with Sheikh Saeed at the London Clinic where he was in for a check-up when he told me Sheikh Zayed had taken over the rulership of Abu Dhabi. When I heard the news I was pleased, it was almost as if my own father had become ruler. Sheikh Zayed had also been like a father to Sheikhs Saeed and Sultan so they accepted his accession to the rulership with equanimity and relief, if not happiness. We all felt Sheikh Zayed was the right man to be at the helm during this critical period in Abu Dhabi's development.

I had known Sheikh Zayed since I was a young boy. In fact my recollections of him go back to the early 1950s when I was just beginning to recognise the people around me and to understand their relationship with me and my family. We grew up in Sheikh Zayed's shadow, as wherever he went my father followed. We were always close to him because of this brotherly relationship. If Sheikh Zayed built a house, he would ask my father to build one nearby so he could call on him for his counsel whenever it was required. When we lived in Muwayje, the small village near Al Ain, he visited my father's house regularly. Although I was living with Sheikh Zayed's wife and son Khalifa at the palace I would also spend time at my father's home when he was there. Sheikh Zayed would come to our majlis where he would be joined by my father, uncles and our neighbours to talk and discuss the events of the day. It seemed to me at the time that he was almost everywhere I turned – in the majlis at the palace, at my father's majlis, outside in the shade of the date palms – and wherever he was he never seemed to be alone. I understood later that it was his great love of Abu Dhabi and its people that kept him so busy in talks, meetings and negotiations. He came to my father's majlis to relax and enjoy the late hours of the day in the companionship of his close friends and advisors. The evenings were a welcome respite after he had received people from the outlying villages and tribes all day long in his own majlis at the palace. So many depended on him and sought his help that he sometimes needed to get away from all the demands and heavy responsibilities he carried on his shoulders.

He was an imposing figure, a very brave and strong man who projected his personality in everything he did, from the confident way he carried his rifle and wore his bandolier to the skilled manner in which he rode his splendid white horse. He simply commanded the respect and attention of those around him by the sheer force of his personality. He worked hard at keeping contact with the people of the area around Al Ain and throughout the rest of the sheikhdom, helping them with their problems whenever he could. To do so he travelled frequently and extensively – accompanied by my father and his other companions – either hunting, visiting neighbouring tribes, exploring tribal settlements or meeting with important people. Sheikh Zayed's name was known by everyone, his reputation as a fair and generous man was equally widespread. Although he did not have much to give in those days he gave anything and everything he had.

He impressed all whom he met, including the intrepid explorer Wilfred Thesiger who, in his book Arabian Sands, describes an encounter with him thus:

> "Some thirty Arabs were sitting under a thorn tree in front of the fort. Our guide pointed and said to me, 'The Sheikh is sitting.' We couched our camels about thirty yards away and walked over, carrying our rifles and camel-sticks. I greeted them and exchanged the news with Zayed. He was a powerfully built man of about thirty with a brown beard. He had a strong, intelligent face, with steady, observant eyes, and his manner was quiet but masterful. He was dressed, very simply in a beige-coloured shirt of Omani cloth, and a waistcoat which he wore unbuttoned. He was distinguished from his companions by his black head-rope, and the way in which he wore his head cloth, falling about his shoulders instead of twisted round his head in the local manner. He wore a dagger and cartridge belt; his rifle lay on the sand beside him.

I had been looking forward to meeting him, for he had a great reputation among the Bedu. They liked him for his easy informal ways and his friendliness, and they respected his force of character, his shrewdness, and his physical strength. They said admiringly: 'Zayed is Bedu. He knows about camels, can ride like one of us, can shoot, and knows how to fight.'"[1]

Sheikh Zayed never tired of meeting the families of those around him as he himself was, and still is, a devoted family man who is extremely sensitive to the feelings of others. He always puts himself in the shoes of those he meets, particularly if they are in need, then goes out of his way to help them if he can. He was very much a father figure to me and my own family – kind, understanding and very generous. As youngsters we always looked up to him as someone we wanted to emulate; when we played war games, each of us pretended to be the brave and courageous Sheikh Zayed. His strength and courage have always been matched by his kindness and compassion, particularly with children for whom he saves a special place in his heart. He goes out of his way to make them feel comfortable by asking their names and speaking with them. When my brothers and I were young we felt this love and returned it tenfold along with our respect and loyalty; and, despite his stature and forceful presence we never feared him as he always treated us with the utmost kindness and concern.

As I grew older I would go to visit him in the palace in Abu Dhabi during his afternoon majlis because I loved to listen to him talk about historical events and current affairs. He was especially skilled at giving advice or instructions from which I benefited a great deal, even in my younger days. He avoided directing his advice or instructions to one person but would speak instead to everyone in the majlis so they could all hear and take advantage of his sagacity.

While he played an important role in the daily lives of the people he was also instrumental in shaping the issues that form the fabric of our recent history. During the early 1950s Sheikh Zayed was so involved with the problems at Buraimi and the settlement of the Saudi claim on the area that he hardly stayed in one location for more than two days. He travelled between tribal settlements taking boundary and frontier surveyors as well as arbitrators to see the disputed area. They travelled mostly by camel, or, when they were fortunate, in vehicles provided by the British. It was a difficult journey past the Liwa to the outlying areas that lay on the border

(1) Thesiger, W.; Arabian Sands; Readers Union Longmans, Green & Co.; London, 1960.

between the Sheikhdom of Abu Dhabi and Saudi Arabia. Sheikh Zayed was instrumental in rallying the tribes around the Ruler of Abu Dhabi at a time when the tribes needed financial assistance. He did not have the financial resources to help them, but he was able to garner their support through the sheer force of his personality and will.

In 1952, just when he needed every rupee he could lay his hands on to feed and clothe his own family, the Saudis offered him forty two million dollars to give up his fight against them and their claim on Buraimi. It was an astounding amount of money – overwhelming to Sheikh Zayed who scarcely had one hundred rupees in his pocket at the time and less than a week's supply of food in his palace. But because he believed in what he was doing and because he is a selfless man, he turned the bribe down proudly. He told the Saudis he did not want their money, he was interested only in the welfare of his people and his homeland. No amount of money could buy his loyalty or change his determination to achieve a peaceful settlement giving the people of Abu Dhabi what was rightfully theirs. The bribe was so incredible that it was registered in the *Guinness Book of World Records* as the highest ever offered to anyone in the world. Sheikh Zayed refused to sell out. He stuck to his guns, and to his principles, maintaining that Al Ain and its environs were part of Abu Dhabi. No amount of money could convince him to sell out. His loyalty never was, never is, and never will be for sale. He is a man of honour who stands proudly for what he believes in.

Similarly, he played a vital role in sorting out the financial complexities surrounding the infant oil industry of the late 1950s and early 1960s. During the oil concession disputes and negotiations there were many power struggles. No one knew who would gain an advantage and come out on top at the negotiating table. Sheikh Shakhbut, who ruled Abu Dhabi at the time, had no previous experience in negotiating these type of agreements, nor did he have advisors upon whom he could depend. The oil companies on the other hand, knew exactly what they were doing and what they wanted because of their previous experience hammering out similar agreements with other Gulf sheikhdoms. Throughout the negotiations Sheikh Zayed was instrumental in getting the Ruler to agree to certain terms that would benefit Abu Dhabi and to reject many that would have been to the sheikhdom's disadvantage. He was very involved in the process and kept abreast of what was happening despite the fact that he was governing the affairs of Al Ain and the eastern part of the sheikhdom and was therefore frequently away from Abu Dhabi town.

Fierce patriotism

Sheikh Zayed believed strongly that the revenues that were being generated as a result of the oil royalties should be used to develop Abu Dhabi. Unfortunately his efforts were often frustrated and his enthusiasm dampened by the Ruler who felt the revenues should be saved in case cash was required for something unexpected such as mounting a defence against an outside threat. He feared that if money was spent on development, it would not be available to deal with an emergency should one arise. Sheikh Zayed, on the other hand, was more interested in growth and development from which he felt all Abu Dhabians would benefit. Having travelled extensively both inside and outside of the Gulf region, seeing the world and meeting all kinds of people, he reckoned that building an infrastructure and educating the local inhabitants were crucial if the sheikhdom was to flourish.

This commitment to development was clearly manifested in his initiatives to modernise Al Ain throughout the early sixties. As governor of the Al Ain area he had full jurisdiction there. He worked diligently and imaginatively to develop the area as much as he could with the limited financial resources available to him at the time. Sheikh Zayed was very keen on improving the agricultural capacity of the area through development of the plantations and he was particularly concerned about stopping the sand from encroaching on the farms and villages. So he established a special department in Al Ain to oversee the expansion of the plantations and green areas. He personally allocated land to the people, encouraging them to establish farms and plant more trees. He helped finance drilling for water wells then gave the farmers pumps run by diesel engines. My father contributed by importing and supplying the motorised pumps, thus enabling the farmers to irrigate the land and make it more productive. In many cases Sheikh Zayed himself paid to have the farms fenced because he knew the people could not afford even the smallest projects to improve their properties. He literally gave them everything they needed to succeed and prosper. From necessity most of what he gave them was borrowed – sometimes borrowed money, sometimes borrowed materials – from merchants and businessmen such as my father. But he felt so strongly that development was the key to the future that he would have done almost anything to see the people had what they needed to improve their lot. He also felt that involving the local people in development efforts and sharing the oil wealth with them would help retain the loyalty of the tribes living here, thus protecting the boundaries of the Sheikhdom of Abu Dhabi from external threats.

At the same time, the British, who were central in getting the oil exported, wanted to see a solid economic foundation in place for the continued exploitation of the vast resources. They wanted development too because they needed it to make the oil industry work properly and profitably. Growth of the oil industry could only be achieved with more qualified staff, better housing, better roads, water resources, electricity, a business community, the list was almost endless. With the Ruler's continued resistance to implement change, the pressure intensified on Sheikh Zayed, his brothers and the ruling family to initiate the development process.

Neighbouring sheikhdoms and countries including Dubai, Qatar, Bahrain and Saudi Arabia knew what kind of revenues were being generated in Abu Dhabi as a result of the oil industry. They were astonished that nothing was being done with the proceeds. Of course it was to their advantage for Abu Dhabi to stay as it was, no development here meant people would continue to turn to them for goods and services. They could not believe their good fortune.

Meanwhile, any one of our neighbours might have successfully claimed rights on Abu Dhabi territories because our defences were weak and the loyalty of the tribes was wavering as the government did little to improve their lot. Had any one of them initiated such a claim the rest would have followed suit and it could well have been a free-for-all with Abu Dhabi being carved up into chunks and divided between its neighbours. Even the thought of this potentiality was completely unacceptable to Sheikh Zayed. He is a fiercely patriotic man who loves his country and its people above all else. He took up arms at the age of fourteen to fight against tribes who were infringing on the territory of Abu Dhabi. He fought against neighbouring countries who claimed our lands. Later, in the 1950s, he used his charm and diplomatic skills to inspire loyalty from the various tribes throughout the eastern area. He negotiated with the British on the one hand and with the Saudis on the other.

When the oil revenues began pouring in he was the one to whom the people turned to initiate development. Unfortunately he lacked the financial resources as well as the power to start the process, much as he would have liked to. He was the youngest of four brothers, the eldest of whom was the Ruler. True, he was an accomplished diplomat with a lot of common sense and a charismatic personality. He also had some influence with his elder brother whom he could sometimes sway or prevail upon to see things differently. But he was not the Ruler. So he remained frustrated by his inability to effect changes that he thought were crucial to the long-term well-being of his country, and his countrymen. His frustration mounted throughout the early and mid-1960s. At the same time he came under increasing pressure to act - from the people of Abu Dhabi, the ruling family itself, the British, and from the intensity of his own convictions. By 1964 the pressure grew so great he could no longer stand by, accepting the status quo, as the revenues from the oil exports accumulated in ever greater amounts. Sheikh Zayed felt it was his duty to act.

Over the next eighteen months he rallied the ruling family around him, including his brothers and cousins who agreed that the situation could not continue as it was, and, with the help of the British, a change in the rulership was finally effected on 6 August 1966. On that memorable day Sheikh Zayed became the Ruler of Abu Dhabi. The former ruler went to Bahrain, then to Iran and finally to Lebanon where he lived for many years.

Starting from scratch

Because his efforts had been frustrated for so long, particularly in the four years prior and had mainly concerned money and financial support, Sheikh Zayed began his rule with an unprecedented act of generosity and goodwill. He opened the palace coffers, literally giving away all the money that had been stockpiled by Sheikh Shakhbut. Incredibly, Sheikh Zayed's generosity was not bounded by the sheikhdom's borders. He announced that anyone in need could come to Abu Dhabi from anywhere in the Trucial States to receive money. Although I was not here at the time, I heard stories of long queues in front of the palace as people waited to get a share of the promised windfall. Everyone was thankful as they were in dire need. With that first act of kindness the amazing transformation began. When I got back from England a little over a year later Abu Dhabi was a completely different place from the one I had left.

As soon as he was in control Sheikh Zayed began taking steps that would bring Abu Dhabi out of the dark ages. The task was enormous. First he needed to put together an entire government and administration because nothing existed at the time. He started from scratch, building the government department by department: water and electricity, finance, municipal planning, police, defence, communication, internal affairs, external affairs, protocol, health, education, a judiciary and more. Here was a man who had never been to school, a man who had lived a nomadic bedouin life since his youth. Yet he both conceived and implemented the ideas that would be the foundation of the entire infrastructure of modern day Abu Dhabi.

Naturally he had to rely on expatriate expertise to a large extent because the local population was simply not qualified yet to complete the tasks that needed to be done. Without schools where they could be taught the majority were still uneducated. So most of the people who ran the government departments initially were brought from elsewhere, seconded from other Arab countries or hired from abroad for their skills. Setting up the framework for the government consumed the first two years of Sheikh Zayed's rule. But that certainly did not mean that nothing else happened during that time. On the contrary, he was actually implementing some of the development plans as the departments were being formed – it all happened in parallel. With the help of his extended family and knowledgeable Abu Dhabians he began executing development plans without delay. In fact a multitude of projects were well underway long before the administration was completely set up.

The inhabitants of Abu Dhabi had been denied the comforts and amenities of progress for a long time, mainly as a result of the decades long tug-of-war between Sheikh Shakhbut and the British authorities. However, in an ironic twist of fate, it was this ongoing conflict which also led to the rule of Abu Dhabi being handed over to a courageous man, Sheikh Zayed, who more than fulfilled our dreams and compensated our people for their suffering during the first sixty-six years of the century.

Record-breaking growth

Now that Sheikh Zayed was at the helm my father's role as his advisor took on even more importance. While he devoted his efforts to helping Sheikh Zayed realise his plans for Abu Dhabi my father needed someone to "mind the shop". So he asked me to come back and learn the family business. I had been looking forward to going on to university but my father was insistent that I return home, thus my return to Abu Dhabi in the autumn of 1967. I was nineteen at the time. When I arrived, a little over a year after Sheikh Zayed had become ruler, the town was changing at a dizzying pace.

As we drove into Abu Dhabi town from the air strip I was amazed at the transformation that had taken place during my absence. The sleepy fishing village I had left was now a bustling construction site. There were trucks, bulldozers, cars and people everywhere – they were doing everything from building roads to laying cables – Abu Dhabi was a hive of activity. There were labour camps everywhere to accommodate the large number of workers required for the countless construction projects. Commercial buildings, government buildings, housing, warehouses, shops – all were going up simultaneously. It was like a scene from the creation of a film set – a whole city was being erected from scratch. I was elated, especially since this change had been so long in coming. Abu Dhabi was finally making its way into the modern day. It would be an exciting time and a completely new phase in the history of the Sheikhdom and its people.

During the next five years the metamorphosis of Abu Dhabi occurred at lightning speed. In some sectors the incredible pace has still not let up. We skipped decades of slow development and simply jumped from the eighteenth century into the twentieth with one giant leap. We went from "no tech" to "high tech" in a matter of a few years. While it took most countries decades to develop communications and transportation systems for example, we did so in a very short time.

We had electricity by 1967, mobile phones in 1972, at roughly the same time, if not before, they were introduced in England, America or anywhere else. The electricity was supplied by diesel generating sets which had been purchased from Hawker Siddeley, one of two British firms who had competed for the contract. The generators were later completely dismantled and replaced by a much larger gas turbine generator which provided thousands of kilowatts of power to Abu Dhabi and Al Ain. Work was undertaken on major projects even before town plans were completely finished. Wherever we turned something was under construction - government buildings, homes, roads, telephone lines. Cables and sewer pipes were laid in deep trenches below ground, while above, street lights were put up on high posts. The Corniche was being built to protect the city against the ravages of the wind and sea. Water desalination plants were constructed; gas pipelines were laid to feed them as well as the electrical generation facilities. The port was being dredged while the airport was under construction and both were completed in 1969.

On the educational side schools went up, teachers were hired, and text books were prepared. Some very fortunate young locals were sent abroad to begin their education immediately so they would be able to make a meaningful contribution to the development of the country in the long term.

Work was ongoing on all fronts and the local inhabitants were participating in almost everything that was being done. Each Abu Dhabian had at least five different jobs or functions in which he played a central role. Members of the ruling family led the way, many of them heading several departments simultaneously. Though not much older than I was at the time, they set up modern day governmental departments and institutions which played a vital role in the development of Abu Dhabi. Among them were Sheikh Hamdan bin Mohammed Al Nahyan heading the Department of Public Works, Sheikh Khalifa bin Zayed Al Nahyan representing the Ruler in Al Ain, Sheikh Tahnoun bin Mohammed Al Nahyan heading the Municipality, Sheikh Sarour bin Mohammed Al Nahyan leading the Department of Justice, and Sheikh Saif bin Mohammed Al Nahyan steering the Health Department. Other prominent members of the community also contributed a great deal: they included Ahmed Khalifa Al Suweidi, the Ruler's Secretary and Advisor, and Mohammed Habroush who headed the Department of Finance.

In 1969 Sheikh Zayed set up an advisory and executive body to help him oversee the administration of all that was going on. The body comprised two councils. The Planning Council was headed by the Ruler himself and included prominent Abu Dhabians such as Khalid Al Yousef, my father, Mahmoud Hassan Juma, Khalifa bin Zayed, and Ahmed Khalifa Al Suweidi. It oversaw infrastructure planning, development and construction. The Water and Electricity Council, led by Hamdan bin Mohammed Al Nahyan, included myself, Khalaf Al Habtour, and Mohammed Bugara among others.

There were so few people who knew anything about administration or management that those who had any experience at all were spread very thin. Everyone who had a skill contributed to his maximum potential. Members of the community participated in a multitude of councils – decision-making, planning, water and electricity, development, municipal affairs – the list seemed endless and yet we had only just begun. Every prominent local businessman sat on at least three or four of these councils while trying to manage his own businesses, build a home and take care of family responsibilities at the same time.

Thankfully, many Abu Dhabians who had left in the previous three decades began to trickle back after 1966. They brought with them a wealth of education, skills and work experience from the host countries – including Saudi Arabia, Qatar, Kuwait and Bahrain – in which they had lived and worked since their departure. They became valued contributors to what was being done at a time when every available hand was needed to help move us forward.

No matter how hard or fast we worked it never seemed to be enough; we were forever running into bottlenecks and problems resulting from the astonishing rate of progress. Rapid development pushed the demand for goods and services through the roof and it jumped from near to nothing to phenomenal levels almost overnight. The incredible influx of foreigners into Abu Dhabi made the building of housing essential, for example, yet it simply could not be put up quickly enough to meet our needs. In 1967 the demand for accommodation was so acute that contracting companies had to build tent camps to house engineers and administrative staff as well as labourers because there was no housing for any of them. As blocks of apartments were finished they were occupied immediately. People moved in before water and electricity services were even connected. Sometimes the impatient tenants were the contractors themselves –

they were in the same boat as everyone else with no suitable place to accommodate their employees.

Our communications capabilities developed relatively quickly but still lagged behind the infrastructure. There were approximately 300 telephones serving a population of about 10,000 in 1967. International Aeradio Limited (IAL) had greatly underestimated the huge level of demand for communications equipment and services, so there was a severe shortage of telephones and related systems. To have a telephone was a rare privilege. Of course the telegraph was also an important innovation of the time, used regularly to transmit and receive overseas messages. Modern communication with other Trucial States, on the other hand, was virtually non-existent. Even within the Sheikhdom of Abu Dhabi there were no telephone links between Abu Dhabi town and Al Ain until late 1969. Our most frequently-used channels of communication were with London, as we turned primarily to the UK to meet the needs of our growing economy in those early years.

Even after the port was opened in 1969, there were still problems receiving and transporting goods. In addition to a lack of off-loading equipment, there was insufficient space at the port to process and store the huge volume of incoming goods. Furthermore, once they were onshore, we did not have enough trucks to move the goods from the port to the city centre where they were needed. The result was severe congestion at the port with ships having to wait to unload and importers not being able to get at their goods.

We worked frenetically to try to provide and maintain all these new things. We built workshops, garages, maintenance sheds; we brought in spare parts. I remember my father ordering 200 car tyres in 1966, his largest order to date. The next year he imported 10,000 tyres - a 5,000 per cent increase! The rate of expansion of businesses, facilities and institutions cannot be adequately described. The small amount of planning that had been done prior to 1966 was, not surprisingly, far too conservative for the rate at which we were growing. We broke all kinds of records for the volume of goods we imported, the amount of work being awarded to contractors and the number of projects that were underway simultaneously in one place.

No room at the inn

One of the ironies of the time was the effect on the Beach Hotel which had been opened by the Bustani family in 1964 but which had never operated anywhere near capacity until 1966. Suddenly it became the only accommodation available in booming Abu Dhabi. It was always fully booked as there was no other place for the tide of visitors to stay. The manager, a Greek named Carentinos, was flooded with requests for accommodation. He added extra beds in all the rooms then put more in the corridors. He even used part of the dining room as sleeping quarters. He would bed latecomers down in the lobby and charge everyone the full rate even though people were staying three or four to a room or sleeping in the most unconventional places. Nevertheless, the visitors actively cultivated his friendship. They feared being put on his black list and possibly being refused a bed at the hotel. Having to spend the night in the back seat of a taxi parked on a secluded area of the beach was a fate they all wished to avoid.

My father and I tried whenever possible to make alternative arrangements for the guests we received on behalf of our principals and the foreign companies with which we dealt. They were either accommodated at the bank manager's house, which sometimes doubled as a private hotel at the time, or we put them in the majlis of our own home because there was nowhere else for them to stay.

While there was a shortage of accommodation for visitors and expatriate workers during the late 1960s and early 1970s, the local inhabitants were moving from their traditional housing to newly constructed homes. The old town, composed almost exclusively of barasti huts made of palm fronds, was being torn down, re-planned and re-zoned for the modern city that would rise like a phoenix from its ashes. As the barasti huts were destroyed to make way for new housing the local inhabitants who had lived in them were compensated handsomely by the government. The money each family was paid to abandon its old dwelling was enough to build a new abode and establish a small business with the remaining funds.

In addition to the monetary compensation, Sheikh Zayed also gave each Abu Dhabian three, and in some cases four, pieces of land. The first was for a home in the residential area, the second was to build a commercial building on one of the main streets in the centre of town, the third was an industrial site meant for a workshop or industrial project of some kind. In addition to these three plots, the people of the Liwa and outlying villages also received a gift of farmland as well as the necessary equipment to cultivate it including machinery, pumps, irrigation systems, even consultants and engineers to provide the necessary advice to make the land productive. All that had to be done was to request assistance from the department of agriculture and they would come to help free of charge.

These land grants were important in teaching many locals how to become landowners and landlords. They generated a fixed income for themselves and their families by building commercial space at the downtown sites then renting them, or leasing the industrial sites which were rarely used by local businessmen at the time as we had few industrial projects or products. People were more often involved with handling the construction and services associated with the development of an infrastructure in Abu Dhabi. In some cases the government built low-cost housing outside town and gave it to the locals, especially those who could not afford to establish a business of their own and thus generate an income. Most of the latter were either employees of the government itself or members of the police and armed forces, who, because of their full-time work commitments, were unable to establish businesses of their own.

The policy of giving each Abu Dhabian property on the island of Abu Dhabi continued until the 1980s when the land eventually ran out. However, most Abu Dhabians can still request and receive a small commercial building which is already in place or a piece of land on the island to build a house. This type of assistance is unknown anywhere else in the world. We are supplied with all the municipal services we require including water and electricity, absolutely free of charge; we do not even pay municipal taxes.

Supportive strategies

Supporting the local people like this was typical of the way in which Sheikh Zayed approached the development of Abu Dhabi. The local people needed this help. They had lived in palm-frond huts for centuries, barely surviving from one year to the next on what they could glean in fish and pearls from the Gulf waters. They had none of the necessary skills to live in a modern society. Sheikh Zayed's foresight was crucial in helping the inhabitants move from the primitive to the present. At the time many local men were leaving their traditional lifestyles as seafarers, shop keepers or bedouin livestock traders. They could see that progress offered opportunities to become involved in trading, importing and exporting, construction and contracting. Unfortunately almost none of them had the education, the experience or the financial resources required to get them started. So the government devised ways to give them the support they needed.

Compensating local inhabitants for their barasti huts was one strategy for putting seed capital directly into the hands of Abu Dhabians. But the government went further than that. It issued a decree saying that all foreign companies had to be either sponsored by, or in partnership with, a local businessman. The ruling gave local entrepreneurs a reason to initiate contact with foreign companies thus expanding their horizons. But more importantly, it ensured that a certain percentage of the profits generated as a result of successful enterprises was re-circulated into the economy through the local businessmen without them having to invest substantial amounts of cash. It gave them an initial income upon which they could build.

The government decreed that no contract would be awarded to any company which was not being sponsored by an Abu Dhabian. They also gave preference to those which were majority owned by local businessmen, thereby making it easier for them to gain a foothold in the market. Additionally, the government made it a policy to order all its supplies locally thus encouraging the local businessmen to set up offices and hire staff to compete in meeting the government's needs. Since the local businessmen were so strongly supported by the government, the banks were quick to extend them credit to help them get firmly established. These far sighted strategies went a long way toward building a solid foundation for an economy which now includes many thriving locally-owned, locally-run companies.

They got local businessmen on their feet, encouraging them to establish themselves and thereby become self-sufficient in the long run rather than reliant on government handouts. The overall success of the plan is indisputable: many of us would not be where we are today had it not been for those early governmental policies.

As might be expected, however, there were inevitable snags along the way. Even the housing compensation scheme had some pitfalls, chief among which was the fact that local Abu Dhabians were simply not accustomed to having or handling large amounts of money. Many wanted to take physical possession of the compensation funds they had been paid by government cheque so it was not uncommon to see local people walking out of the banks carrying cardboard boxes full of cash on their heads. Some spent their money wisely building new homes and getting involved in entrepreneurial ventures. Others, however, marched directly to a car showroom and used the money to pay cash for a brand new late-model vehicle which would be virtually worthless after they had driven it in the sand around Abu Dhabi for six months. It took some time for the local inhabitants to understand the value of money and material goods. Their first impulse was to squander their new-found wealth on short-term benefits rather than using it to generate long-term security.

Similarly, the local businessmen were handicapped to some degree as they had no previous education, experience or training that equipped them to run a modern business or company. To compensate for this shortcoming most hired expatriates to manage their business while they themselves focused on the marketing and public relations aspects. The use of expatriate expertise was a necessity given the situation at the time. However, it sometimes meant that local entrepreneurs took longer to acquire much needed business skills than it would have had they been more directly involved in the day-to-day management of their companies. By confining their role to marketing and public relations activities they missed the opportunity to learn broader business management and administration principles. Of course they were also hampered somewhat by the fact that many could devote only a few hours daily to their own businesses while they were employed by the government on a full-time basis trying to help get Abu Dhabi itself up and running.

Many local businessmen went into construction because of the huge growth in this sector. Unfortunately only a few persevered, eventually prospered and made a name for themselves. The same happened with road construction, cabling and electrification. Many others went into transportation and trucking which required few administrative skills. An inexperienced local with limited technical knowledge could manage a trucking business comparatively easily. Still, the money losers outnumbered the money makers in some cases simply because the former did not have even the minimal expertise required to run a successful operation. Undaunted, the government persisted in its policy of involving local inhabitants thus ensuring they benefited financially from the development process while they also learned the fundamentals of good business management. Sheikh Zayed was very keen on channelling the oil wealth down to everyone thereby making his generosity work toward the future well-being of our society as a whole. He helped Abu Dhabians directly with financial support and indirectly through government policies. Despite the occasional hiccup, his efforts eventually paid off. The result has been the sharing of Abu Dhabi's oil wealth amongst the many rather than just the few.

In the driver's seat

While all of this was going on around me I was equally busy learning the family business and trying to take advantage of every opportunity that arose.

Initially, my father gave me responsibility for the automotive parts shop he had opened some years before. When I took it over he had already formalised agency agreements with Mercedes Benz and Chrysler cars, Michelin and Firestone tyres, Shell lubricants and petroleum products, Hawker Siddeley, NCR and BICC, a well-known British cable company. He had also opened a small travel agency which was the general sales agent for Middle East Airlines and soon to be the representative of Swissair - an agreement which I completed in my early days with the company. In addition, he had built six small shops to house the various businesses on Sheikh Hamdan Street. Hamdan Street comprised, at the time, a short stretch of the hard-surfaced road Sheikh Zayed had had built during the absence of Sheikh Shakhbut in 1961, bordered by a row of small shops and houses on either side. We certainly never dreamed then that in less than twenty-five years it would become a busy downtown thoroughfare hemmed by high rises and hotels.

My father's companies were expanding in leaps and bounds, but with the amount of time he devoted to assisting Sheikh Zayed he was not able to handle them on his own. He had five employees including myself, though I was still too inexperienced to take over the business completely. I also looked even younger than my nineteen years. I grew a beard, which helped somewhat, though many people still refused to take me seriously despite the fact that my father left me in charge for months at a time while he was away with Sheikh Zayed. Of course I had to make decisions in his absence even though some company representatives felt I was too young to do business with them. But there were many others who wished to see me succeed: they taught me more about business than I could ever have learnt in a school. They gave me astute advice and guided me in the right direction for which I remain grateful to this day. While I took advantage of their expertise I also managed to hire people who were older and more knowledgeable than myself. They too helped me run things properly. Together we instituted management systems for sales, accounting, inventory control and administration, none of which we had previously.

We modernised and expanded the business changing our focus from spare parts to the importation of more vehicles, both new Mercedes and Chrysler cars as well as second-hand Bedford trucks and new Mercedes trucks. In 1965 my father imported four Mercedes cars, two were sold, one he used himself and the fourth broke down and could not be repaired. Two years later the demand for cars was so great that we could not keep up with it. Sometime in 1967 my father found out through a company representative that Mercedes had thirteen limousines – the 600 type – available for immediate shipment. My father took all thirteen, in addition to his regular order of thirty-five smaller vehicles, despite the fact that there were still no roads to drive on in Abu Dhabi. When the limos arrived, however, they were all sold immediately We fitted them with balloon tyres so they could be driven anywhere in town; some even crossed the desert to Al Ain, a trip for Land Rovers and specialised vehicles which the re-fitted Mercedes limousines made successfully nevertheless.

Business was booming. Everything we imported was sold on the spot. But more incredible than the growth in demand was the way in which many purchases were made – the vehicles we imported were being snapped up from the beach. Most goods that came from Europe took about three months to get to Abu Dhabi; the city was not a regular port of call on the shipping lanes as there were no port facilities at the time. Once they got here the goods, including vehicles, were off-loaded from the freighters onto flat barges about three or four kilometres offshore. The barges were then towed by tug right to the beach close to where the clock tower roundabout is now located on the Corniche. Wooden ramps were leant against the vessels and the cars driven off onto the beach where they invariably got stuck in the soft sand and had to be pushed out. As I stood on the beach supervising the whole affair customers would approach, asking me the price of the vehicles. If they found the price acceptable, and the vehicle had not yet been sold, they would stuff bundles of cash into my hands, slip into the driver's seat and drive away in their new car. There was no paperwork involved, no documentation or licensing, not even an invoice - people just handed me the money, took the keys and drove off. Such was the frenzied buying spree fuelled by the oil wealth, some of which had finally found its way into the hands of the people. The off-loading of cars and most other consumer goods on the beach continued until the first basic port facilities were completed at Mina Zayed in 1969.

Even in those early days our company was not limited solely to the automotive industry. We were involved in many other different areas including electrification; road, highway and building construction; and of course the travel business, despite the paucity of flights landing and departing at the time. There were only a few Fokkers, acquired by Gulf Aviation, and the Middle East Viscounts planes, using Abu Dhabi's primitive airstrip. The flights were always full so reservations had to be made well in advance to travel anywhere.

Administering these various business interests was extraordinarily difficult as we lacked both the infrastructure and a full complement of experienced staff to keep things running smoothly. The problems we encountered were common to any organisation, private or public, that was trying to get things done in Abu Dhabi in the late 1960s. Expatriate employees, for example, had to be hired because there was little skilled labour available locally. However, the hiring process itself was fraught with complications not the least of which was where to accommodate people once they arrived. The innumerable obstacles were frustrating for everyone in the business community particularly since the government was being so generous in awarding contracts to local businessmen. Getting the contracts was easy. But fulfilling them, in the face of hurdles which included a lack of human resources as well as materials, was extremely challenging. Still, we did our best and in most cases were successful in getting the job done.

Chapter 7

Birth of a Nation

Born of necessity

In January 1968, the British announced their intention to withdraw from all territories east of Suez, including Abu Dhabi and the surrounding sheikhdoms. Having been a controlling force in the area for more than 170 years they were ready to relinquish their hold primarily for financial reasons, although there was a political component to the withdrawal as well. In Egypt, Jamal Abdul Nasser was calling for the Arab world to resist colonisation, encouraging his Arab brothers to fight imperialism. Meanwhile, the Yemenis had forced the British out of Aden, which the latter had colonised for over one hundred years. Furthermore, the British economy was in poor shape, weakened by labour unrest, frequent strikes and other problems. It was simply no longer in their best interests to maintain their position here and they were anxious to extricate themselves sooner rather than later. They had no desire to replicate the Yemeni situation and could ill afford to maintain warships, troops and administrators in the area given their ailing economy. Their decision to withdraw would have far-reaching long-term effects on the political and economic development of the Trucial States. It would also have a negative impact on the British trade position here.

The timing of the announcement could not have been worse for British manufacturers for whom the area was a significant market. Even as early as 1968 the growth in demand for goods and materials had surpassed their most optimistic forecasts. But when the British government decided to pull out, it also pulled the plug on the virtual monopoly British companies had on this rapidly developing market, a market which they had cultivated for a long time. As soon as Her Majesty's Government announced its intention to leave, competitors from Japan, France, Germany, Italy and the United States swooped in on the British monopoly and the market they had created. Consumers soon began moving away from British goods as better quality and more innovative products became available from other suppliers. The Japanese, for example, offered smaller more compact cars equipped with air conditioning. They also produced more affordable four-wheel drive vehicles as well as portable generators which were easier to move than similar British machines. By using better technologies, non–British companies found a ready market for their goods in Abu Dhabi and neighbouring sheikhdoms.

At about the same time, British Prime Minister Wilson began improving relations with the Israeli Government of Golda Meir, overtures that most Arabs felt were an insult to the Palestinian cause. Calls to boycott British manufacturers soon lessened the demand for a wide range of their products including vehicles from Land Rover, Austin Morris and Vauxhall among others. As a result, the British did not benefit as much as they might have from the phenomenal growth of the market here during the latter part of the 1960s and the early 1970s. The few British companies still working in the area - the telephone company among them - found it more difficult to carry on with business as usual as competition came in from all sides and the effects of the boycott took their toll.

The telephone company imported all its phones from the UK; with better technologies becoming available elsewhere, it could no longer compete. Furthermore, it simply could not meet the demand of the market here. This situation prompted the Abu Dhabi government, in the early 1970s to buy out the British shareholder completely and re-capitalise the company. First called Emirtel, and later renamed Etisalat, the company went on to become the pride of the United Arab Emirates. It continues to be the envy of the Arab world because it is highly technical, very profitable and eminently well-run. It is a leader in its industry, providing excellent products and services, some of which are still unavailable in many countries.

British withdrawal from the Trucial States meant the latter would be left without the umbrella of protection that had guarded the coastal area against external aggressors since 1892. That opened the door for any one of our neighbours to claim territories that were ours. Sheikh Zayed immediately recognised the danger. He proposed that the Trucial States form a union to prevent the sheikhdoms from being swallowed up by one or more of their bigger neighbours. The idea of unifying the sheikhdoms was not a new one. Sheikh Zayed bin Khalifa had thought of pursuing unification in the late 1800s and, more recently, the British had also tried to encourage the ruling sheikhs to move in that direction. In fact, a council of the Trucial States' ruling sheikhs had been formed in 1952. The British had been less than successful in their efforts to persuade the rulers to federate, however, so they were no closer to unification in January 1968 than they had been sixteen years earlier. The difficult job of pulling the disparate parties together and demonstrating the benefits of federation fell to Sheikh Zayed. While he was completely convinced of the advantages of such a union, the other rulers were somewhat less enthusiastic.

The men Sheikh Zayed had to sway were the same ones with whom he and other members of the Abu Dhabi ruling family had been in conflict for years, if not generations. The very nature of the region and the tribal structure of our society meant they were predisposed to resisting federation. Initially, the other ruling sheikhs were mistrustful and sceptical – not surprisingly as they stood to lose a great deal of personal power with the formation of a federation. They certainly were nowhere near agreeing to a union simply because the British were pulling out and they might have to face unknown problems as a result.

Sheikh Zayed had an enormously challenging task ahead of him if he was to get them to accept his proposal. Nevertheless, by compromising on the frontier issue that had simmered between Abu Dhabi and Dubai since the Ghanada incident in 1946, Sheikh Zayed managed to convince Sheikh Rashid bin Said, the Ruler of Dubai, to agree to join forces. Amazingly, their agreement was signed within a month of the British having made their declaration to withdraw. Within the following two weeks the five other rulers of the emirates which now comprise the UAE, as well as the rulers of Qatar and Bahrain, had met and agreed in principle to form a federation. The details of the structure, rules and scope of the federation still had to be hammered out however. Building a proposal to which all the rulers could agree proved challenging.

In addition to his own internal affairs, Sheikh Zayed now took it upon himself to finalise the agreement between the neighbouring rulers - including those of Qatar and Bahrain. He worked tirelessly, day and night, travelling from one end of the country to the other meeting the rulers, both separately and collectively, try to find terms and conditions acceptable to everyone. He felt the federation was crucial to the continued well-being of the peoples of the region and nothing would deter him from achieving his goal.

Abu Dhabians were too preoccupied improving their own lot - building and outfitting businesses and homes - to give Sheikh Zayed's efforts the attention they deserved. We were busy bettering our standard of living and catching up with those who had surpassed us in creature comforts and business successes. While Sheikh Zayed drove back and forth, meeting, cajoling, reassuring and pouring his heart and soul into making the federation a reality, we in Abu Dhabi sat back and watched, not fully comprehending why he was working so hard on this union. We were quite happy with the status quo. We had access to the financial resources we needed to develop an infrastructure for our economy. We were building Abu Dhabi, increasing our own material well-being as individuals and providing the next generation with the education required to continue what we had started. We were far too focused on our own immediate needs to pay much attention to the longer term implications of a federation.

Yet Sheikh Zayed persisted. He was a tireless advocate, so committed that he would go all the way to the Qatari border to meet the ruler there then double back the same day to meet the ruler of Dubai. He zig-zagged across the region and flew to Bahrain. He constantly invited the ruling sheikhs and emirs to meet, pushing them to forget the past, encouraging them to think ahead to the disastrous consequences that might materialise should their efforts at federation fail. The British were leaving, that was clear. Without their protection, the area was extremely vulnerable.

At times Sheikh Zayed despaired of realising his vision of a federation, but he never gave up. He was so convinced of our vulnerability without the British that, in a last ditch attempt to buy time, he even offered them money – twenty five million pounds a year – just to protect the area a little longer, at least until he managed to conclude the all-important federal agreement. But the British were resolute, they wanted out. After two and half years of hard work, negotiations became more difficult. Then, Bahrain opted out of the proposed federation, declaring her independence in August 1971; Qatar followed suit about two weeks later. With only a few months remaining before the British protectorate was to end, the remaining seven sheikhs re-doubled their efforts.

Thankfully, God in his wisdom always prevails, sometimes directing us to do things we might not fully comprehend even as we do them; the results can be astonishing. Perhaps it was such divine intervention which finally inspired the ruling sheikhs. In any event, on 2 December 1971, as a result of the constant meetings, writing and persistence of Sheikh Zayed, the federation of the United Arab Emirates was proclaimed. Shortly thereafter, Sheikh Zayed bin Sultan Al Nahyan was elected president of the newly formed nation.

Federation proves challenging

A new era dawned with the birth of the United Arab Emirates. Sheikh Zayed and the rulers of the other emirates worked closely together to form a federal government. Our local government, which included a prime minister, departmental ministers and so on, had to be restructured better to meet the needs of the fledgling federation. We had hardly established our own systems in Abu Dhabi than the whole exercise began once more. New federal ministries were formed to replace some of the old departments and run the affairs of all seven emirates. We went back to the drawing board, again building most things from scratch. We learnt as we went. Some people received formal training, others simply got an education on the job, but either way we had to gain quickly the skills required to make the newly federated state successful.

The years immediately after federation were difficult because we all had to learn new jobs either in trading, diplomacy, services or technical areas with which we were completely unfamiliar. It was particularly challenging in Abu Dhabi as we found ourselves having to oversee all seven federated emirates rather than just one. Considering the enormity of the task and the tools we had available at the time we succeeded quite admirably.

Like my associates, I contributed wherever I could. Initially, that meant joining the diplomatic corps and taking an intensive training programme to equip me with the necessary skills for an ambassadorial position. In the early days, Abu Dhabi's main obstacle to development had been a lack of human resources. In fact, until very recently, we have always had to cope with a shortage of trained and educated local people. In 1971 the problem was acute. We needed highly skilled and informed UAE nationals to take on jobs as ministers, ambassadors and high ranking officials, representing not only their own territories, as they may have done before federation, but also the newly created federal state of the United Arab Emirates. Beyond filling the senior posts we had to establish additional ministries, departments and affiliated sections throughout the seven emirates to coordinate and implement all the work that needed to be done. Fortunately, there were qualified people from Dubai, Ras al Khaimah, Sharjah and the northern emirates who were sufficiently educated to step into some roles immediately. They had schools long before we did in Abu Dhabi and were therefore more likely to have received at least a basic education. The federal government drew heavily on this pool of qualified, educated nationals which helped to some extent. Nevertheless, we were still forced to import additional personnel to help run government departments, ministries and educational facilities.

The first cabinet comprised ministers who were in their early thirties, quite young in comparison to government representatives in most developed countries. Furthermore, most of these inexperienced young men were stepping into newly created positions that required them to set up entire ministries virtually on their own. The process of forming the requisite government bodies - challenging and time consuming though it was - eventually bore fruit. Once they were established, however, we had to overcome an even greater hurdle - convincing the citizens of the UAE to accept a form of government which was completely foreign to them.

Tribal roots

When the nation was formed in 1971, the people here were not accustomed to dealing with a government bureaucracy, public institutions or large organisations. When they had a problem or a special need they simply went to their tribal chief or ruler for help. Getting the inhabitants to trust the government to take care of them, to look upon the president as their leader and the head of the new country, and to see themselves as citizens of the United Arab Emirates was incredibly difficult. It meant changing an entire way of life and thinking which had been passed down from one generation to the next for hundreds of years.

Mobilising the loyalty of the nomadic desert tribes was especially daunting. Formal education had previously been completely unknown to them. They moved from one location to another with the seasons, depending on the availability of pasture for their livestock. Their children never went to school, the elders simply passed on what they knew to the next generation. They were trained from an early age to be on the alert at all times in anticipation of the tribal conflicts that were so much a part of their lives – they were warriors by necessity not by choice. Apart from being able to worship, defend their territories and tend their goats and camels, they knew very little.

Their religion and culture dictated that their allegiance must lie with the two beings who would care for and protect them – God above and the chief of their tribe here on earth. They were steadfast, unwavering in their devotion to God, their tribe and their tribal chief; there were no ministries, no departments, no government, no central authority to whom they were accountable. Nor was there a sense of belonging to a wider community other than the tribal group. Members of individual tribes kept to themselves relying on each other for safety and protection against rivals whose territories bordered their own.

On the other hand, the allegiance of the tribes themselves changed with the wind depending on who was best able to provide them with whatever financial support and protection they needed. One year they might be loyal to the Ruler of Dubai and the next, when the Ruler of Abu Dhabi helped them, it was to the latter that they pledged their allegiance. They switched from one provider to another because their nomadic way of life made it extremely difficult to sustain themselves on their own. They derived only a meagre income from their livestock and the wood they cut in the wilderness and sold in the coastal settlements.

The situation of the more sedentary tribes, who lived for the most part in small towns and settlements throughout the territories of the

Emirates, was similar in one fundamental sense - after God, their members were devoted to their tribe and its chief only. Federation brought with it a foreign system; one which implied a radically different social structure. The tribal society afforded people immediate access to their primary protector. Now the leader seemed so far removed, everything was different, unknown and, probably for many of them, a little frightening. They disliked the artificial barriers now separating them from the seat of power. Before they would accept the new situation they needed tangible proof that the central government system would work for them, meet their needs and take their interests to heart. The newly-formed institutions and government bodies had to show the inhabitants they were worthy of the people's trust and confidence.

In addition to cultural barriers there were other factors which served to separate us one from another. Under British protection we had been isolated from the outside world and, before federation, each of the sheikhdoms had been, to all intents, a totally independent entity. Prior to the arrival of motorised vehicles, travel from one sheikhdom to the next was undertaken only when absolutely necessary as it was dangerous, arduous and time consuming. It became somewhat less so with the advent of four-wheel drives but then border restrictions impeding such trips were implemented. When travelling between Abu Dhabi and Dubai, or Dubai and Sharjah, or Sharjah and Ras al Khaimah, for example, a passport and proper vehicular authorisation from the police were required from about 1959 onwards. While they were travelling on dirt tracks rather than proper roads, the driver and occupants of any vehicle crossing a border had to produce their passports for stamping at the checkpoints. Those without passports - and many people did not have them because they were rarely needed - simply did not travel between sheikhdoms. Even by the late sixties it would have been unusual for someone from Abu Dhabi ever to have visited Ras al Khaimah as travel was not nearly as convenient or as easy as it is today. Before the formation of the UAE in 1971 the inhabitants of the seven member emirates had had little, if any, personal contact other than during the skirmishes resulting from territorial disputes. Since there was no mass communication to speak of - no newspapers, radio, or television - their isolation from each other was virtually complete, despite the fact they were separated by only short distances - 150 kilometres from Abu Dhabi to Dubai, 15 kilometres from Dubai to Sharjah and 80 kilometres from Sharjah to Ras al Khaimah.

Tangible benefits
To assist in the process of bringing the populace across the country

into the federal fold, the ruling sheikhs devoted an enormous amount of time to meeting personally with their constituents. They informed them of the benefits of federation. They told them that while it was good to be loyal to their tribal chief, they must also understand that he was now supported by a government and a country that also needed their loyalty. Sheikh Zayed himself visited many of the tribes in the outlying areas, living among them for days at a time, convening meetings, talking with them, telling them what was going on and helping them meet their day-to-day needs. He wanted to go much further than simply getting them to accept the new state, however. His long-term objective was for them to become useful citizens who made significant contributions to the economy either by getting an education, farming, or working in the oil industry. In keeping with this goal tribe members were often recruited by the military or the police. The government also strongly encouraged the oil companies to take them on as labourers, guards and drivers because Sheikh Zayed felt everyone, even the less skilled and poorly educated, should benefit in some way from the development that was taking place.

Despite the benefits, it was difficult for people to forget about the old ways and embrace the new. They had to set aside hundreds of years of tribal traditions that revolved around defending their home territory against neighbouring tribes. Now these neighbours were no longer their foes but their countrymen. Making the transition from tribal loyalty to a sincere belief in the new country took a lot of effort but eventually it was achieved.

Involving the tribal chiefs was crucial to the whole transition process. Some were appointed to the Federal Council, others were given important positions in the ministries. They gained valuable knowledge about the system which they then passed on to the members of their tribes. But the most convincing arguments for the new government were the tangible benefits to the populace in the form of assistance, education, electrical power and continuing development in a host of other areas.

Sheikh Zayed took an interest in all the major development projects underway across the country but he was most strongly committed to those involving agriculture and forestation. His main objective was to minimise the negative effects of sand movement and desertification. He wanted to create an agricultural industry that would eventually allow the UAE to be almost completely self-sufficient in agricultural produce. When we look around today we see the results of his continuing efforts in this field. The towns and cities throughout the Emirates abound with greenery, especially in Abu Dhabi and on some of the islands - there have been an estimated nine million trees planted since 1966. The transformation is almost beyond belief.

The other major project the President and Ruler took a great interest in was the development of the urban areas and the resettlement of the nomadic bedouin who used to migrate continuously in search of fodder for their livestock. Rather than trying to relocate these nomads to the larger towns Sheikh Zayed built them houses, mosques and shops in their own areas and divided the empty desert into small farms for them. He financed the bedouin farming efforts, even helping them market their produce by setting up a co-operative society to purchase their produce and sell it in bulk to wholesalers or retail to individual consumers. This was a huge boon to the bedouin who, at the outset, had even less experience in selling produce than they had in growing it. The system removed the selling burden from the new farmers, giving them a ready market for whatever they produced. A solid foundation was laid for the UAE's fledgling agricultural sector while the bedouin people began to develop trust in the new system.

Accomplishments such as these eventually persuaded people that the newly formed government could be trusted to do the right thing. After much persuasion and coaxing, inhabitants across the country started going to the various government bodies set up to respond to their problems and needs. Their way of life changed in a very short time as they became more integrated into the developing society of the UAE. It is rewarding now to see many of the younger members of the nomadic tribal groups studying, working in technical positions, holding jobs in government institutions and contributing in important ways to the continuing growth and development of our country. Seeing these young adults today one can hardly believe that less than twenty-five years ago they were living in goat-hair tents in the desert.

While the seven emirates were working together to become a truly cohesive country, each also followed its own unique path toward development. In Abu Dhabi we had a lot more ground to make up than some of our more fortunate federal partners.

Shortly after federation, the local government in Abu Dhabi saw a need to evaluate the land grant programme which had been in place for several years. Numerous Abu Dhabians had clearly benefited from the government gift of several pieces of land. Others, however, especially those who lived away from Abu Dhabi island in the desert tribal camps, were uninterested in building, leasing or doing anything at all with the land they had been given. Land development took time, not to mention considerable effort, and they had no idea where to begin. Besides, they were more interested in ready cash than construction, buildings and leases. Rather than building on the land as the government had intended, many found buyers who were more affluent, business-minded and able to afford to build on the lots. So they sold their land at low prices - 10,000 dirhams for a prime piece. This was excellent value for the buyers. The sellers, however, used the cash immediately to improve their standard of living, leaving them without a secure source of income in the long term. Once the cash ran out they were right back to where they had started. This prompted the government to establish a ruling whereby those who had been given land were allowed to lease it to expatriates who could then build on it for commercial or personal purposes. However, if after four years the local landowner was in a better financial position he could then negotiate with the lessor to repossess it.

In keeping with the spirit of the regulations, which covered dealings with expatriates only, I decided to use the experience I had gained in business to help some of the new landowners. I contacted a number of those who owned adjoining pieces of land - about eighteen in all - and proposed the following: I would lease the land from them for building purposes; after eight years I would terminate the lease agreement and they could take back the land along with whatever I had built on it. During the leasing period, which included two years for construction, I paid them rent for the land, negotiated financing and contracted a construction company to build thirty-six villas on the lots.

The demand for accommodation remained high, even though housing construction had been going full tilt for several years. I was able to repay the loan, settle with the contracting company, maintain the rental payments to the landowners and still make a reasonable profit. At the end of eight years the property owners got back their land, complete with villas which they could then rent immediately. It was a "no lose" situation. Had these people sold the pieces of land eight years earlier they would have received only 20,000 dirhams. Now they had something that would continue to generate an income for many years. I, on the other hand, was able to make a good return on my investment within a relatively short period of time. Having done so, I became somewhat of a celebrity among the bedouin whom I had helped. Even now, when I meet one of those initially reluctant landlords, they thank me for what I did. Today the properties still produce sufficient income to support them and their children. Of course it was challenging and somewhat risky, but I am pleased to have helped these people rather than taking advantage of them as some others did.

Winning over the world

In addition to overseeing the internal affairs of our new country by instituting pilot projects and ensuring a relatively smooth transition from the old ways to the new, Sheikh Zayed also focused considerable energy on external relations which were equally important at the time.

The first major foreign affairs goal Sheikh Zayed set was to achieve world recognition and acceptance of the United Arab Emirates as an independent state. It was a formidable task as only a few years before hardly anyone had even heard of us. We sprang up from nowhere, still relatively undeveloped yet aspiring to catch up quickly with the rest of the world. To most people outside the Gulf region, other than the few who had visited here, we were an unknown people with a mysterious culture and a nomadic way of life. Even our Arab neighbours to the north were unfamiliar with us before we became a country in 1971. I personally experienced just how little people knew of us when, in 1969, I asked for the hand of a lovely Lebanese woman in marriage.

I had met her on a business trip to Beirut, following which we had corresponded regularly. After a year-long exchange of letters she had agreed to my proposal of marriage. Once I had her assent I went to Beirut to seek permission from her father. Not only did he express shock and surprise that someone from an unknown country should propose to marry his daughter, he totally rejected my suit on the grounds that a young woman, born in Egypt and educated in Lebanon, would not survive the primitive life of a nomad in the desert of Abu Dhabi. I was deflated but determined. It took two long years of lobbying, and a visit to Abu Dhabi by her mother and brother, finally to convince her father that life here was not as primitive as he had thought. But it was only on the testimony of his wife and son, who saw for themselves that we were totally civilised, that he finally agreed to give me his daughter's hand in marriage.

Over time, just as I had managed to win over my future father-in-law, Sheikh Zayed's diplomatic efforts began to win over the world. We started attending important meetings abroad and participating in international conferences. The acceptance we desired so fervently, however, was not easy to get. It took many years, almost a decade of diligent diplomacy, before we were finally accepted by most major industrialised countries. This was considerably longer than many others who had simply declared their independence and were almost immediately acknowledged as sovereign states. The decade-long push for recognition also involved careful navigation through the politically turbulent waters of the Middle East.

In October 1973, just as we looked forward to a relatively peaceful period of economic and political consolidation, a fourth Arab-Israeli war broke out. Suddenly we found ourselves in a crisis. We had remained untouched by previous Arab-Israeli wars, as we were somewhat distant, both physically as well as philosophically, from the conflicts. By 1973 our situation had changed radically. We were a small new federation trying to gain world acceptance and recognition. Being newly established, the goodwill and support of our closest neighbours, as well as other Islamic states, were crucial to our very survival as a nation. It was vital that we nurture positive relationships within our region before turning our efforts to the rest of the international community. The Arab-Israeli conflict escalated quickly and the Arab community worldwide contemplated various measures to show its solidarity against the Israelis. There was pressure on the large oil-producing Arab countries to stop exporting oil to those countries which supported Israel. All eyes were directed to the Gulf region, the location of the world's richest oil reserves and the source of oil supplies to the West. Though still struggling to develop our small nation and have it recognised on the world stage, the people of the United Arab Emirates, under the leadership of Sheikh Zayed, made a bold move. In support of our Arab brothers who were engaged with Israel in 1973, Sheikh Zayed was the first Arab head of state to take the courageous decision to stop the export of oil completely. Saudi Arabia followed suit immediately.

During the war, which was very short and equally intense, the Egyptians and Syrians regained some of their lost territories from Israel. Regrettably, however, many lives were lost on all sides. The impact in the Gulf was more economic than it was political.

As a direct result of the oil embargo to the West - the primary purpose of which was to show Arab solidarity - the price of oil skyrocketed. No sooner was the brief war over than the oil began to flow again and we found ourselves in a tidal wave, awash with money. The income of the government soared with the increased oil revenues, the majority of which were funnelled right back into the economy. Land prices skyrocketed to unheard-of levels, even by today's standard, and the prices of goods, materials and services went through the roof along with the increasing revenues. The UAE found itself in the midst of a boom.

In 1973 we imported two or three times the amount of goods we had in 1971. Building codes changed, increasing the height limit for multi-storey buildings from six floors to thirteen, so additional building materials were required. More trucks and heavy machinery were needed to expand and enlarge the road network that was under construction at the time. The seven sheikhdoms that now comprise the UAE had never seen such clamour and development in their entire history. The explosion in growth was not without drawbacks however.

Sheikh Zayed was a strong advocate of Arabism, a commitment he had clearly demonstrated by turning off the oil taps in support of Egypt and Syria. He tried as much as possible to maintain positive relationships with our Arab brothers throughout the region. In one case, with the Saudis, he managed to patch a relationship torn by seemingly endless territorial disputes. After King Faisal assumed power in 1964 and Sheikh Zayed became Ruler of Abu Dhabi two years later, mutual friendship, admiration and respect between the two leaders helped open direct negotiations on boundary issues. In 1974 they signed a frontier agreement that finally buried the hatchet in the one hundred and seventy-year-long struggle over the Buraimi area. Immediately thereafter Saudi Arabia recognised the United Arab Emirates. Unfortunately the agreement surrendered to Saudi Arabia a large chunk of oil-producing territory, including a slice of the Abu Dhabi mainland and the port of Khor Al Udaid, and separated us from our Qatari neighbours who then became completely encircled by Saudi Arabia.

Apart from this type of compromise for the sake of good relations, Sheikh Zayed tried to remain non-partisan in the affairs of the region - no mean task in the politically volatile Middle East. Even maintaining neutrality required a lot of energy, strategising and manoeuvreing which did not preclude somehow becoming involved whether we wished to or not. Sadly, we lost our minister of foreign affairs who was shot in the Abu Dhabi airport in 1977 while escorting the Syrian minister of foreign affairs who was leaving the country after an official visit. The attempt was on the life of the latter but it was our minister, His Excellency Saif Al Ghubash, who was murdered in cold blood when the assassin missed his target. Our ambassador to France, His Excellency Khalifa Al Mubarek, was assassinated in Paris in 1982 for reasons we still do not fully understand. There was also an attempt on our ambassador in Kuwait. Thankfully he survived the attack, shocked, but unhurt. We found these incidents both horrifying and hard to understand. We had not taken up arms, nor did we have reason to quarrel with anyone outside our borders. Yet it seemed others were entangling us in political games for which we had no desire.

Our wise ruler knew that as a young country we must maintain amicable relationships with other nearby Arab nations, our Muslim brothers worldwide, and our important international trading partners regardless of their nationality or their religion. It was crucial that we not become isolated through indifference to the events around us, especially in a world that had become so small as a result of global communication. It was, and still is, vital that we contribute in a meaningful way as a member of the international community. In keeping with the teachings of Islam Sheikh Zayed welcomed non-Arabic speaking Muslims from the sub-continent and across Asia. As a supporter of Arab solidarity he invited the participation of our Arab neighbours in the development of the UAE. Expatriates from across Asia and the Middle East flooded into the Emirates to take advantage of the opportunities here. There were Indian and Pakistani merchants, engineers, electricians, masons and mechanics as well as teachers seconded from Egypt, Jordan, Sudan, Palestine, Lebanon and Syria, for example. Because we had a common religion and, for the most part, a common language we felt we were dealing with friends not foes. In the case of our neighbours we shared the same Arab perspective on life and the world. Or so we believed. Unfortunately, we found to our dismay that it took more than such commonalities to build a solid foundation for trustworthy relationships. We experienced many problems in our dealings with expatriate workers whatever their religion, their language or their culture.

Three hundred tons of olives

We were accustomed to relying on our word as our bond when we made agreements or business deals. None of us went to the trouble of writing things down; contracts, agreements and business deals were sealed with a man's word. When a promise was made we expected it to be kept. We had no courts or justice system because they were never needed. If there was a dispute or misunderstanding the members of the tribe would resolve it amongst themselves rather than use a court or a judge. However, most of the problems that needed to be solved in bygone days were minor when compared to those we encountered as we joined the world community. We all thought people lived as we did using tribal and ethical systems to resolve issues. We found to our dismay and disappointment that this was not the case - not everyone believed in the same principles. Because we were so trusting and naive we never documented agreements, and so almost all of us lost money one way or another as a result. Under the circumstances it was hardly surprising that we fell victim to people who took advantage of our ignorance and vulnerability.

Some local people sponsored or acted as loan guarantors for virtual strangers who had come to them for help. Some opened businesses and gave full management and signing authority to a foreign partner. We acted in good faith, never thinking our partners would abuse the privileges we had given them. But apparently many of our partners did not share our commitment to honesty in business dealings. Consequently, there were many abuses which often cost the local businessmen dearly. Some expatriates, for example, emptied company accounts then disappeared, leaving their local partners liable for debts and commitments. Some employees learned a new skill or job in the space of a year then left their original sponsor to form partnerships with their sponsor's competitors. Others fled the UAE with large amounts of cash but left behind unpaid debts and commitments. Even the government, members of the ruling family and prominent businessmen fell prey to these criminal activities. In hindsight what happened was a blessing in disguise - it taught us to be watchful and aware and not as trusting as was our custom in the past. It put us on the alert. At the time, however, it was devastating for the victims.

Corrupt businessmen from abroad made the UAE a dumping ground for damaged and unsaleable goods which they could not dispose of elsewhere. A lot of merchants in Abu Dhabi and the rest of the emirates purchased merchandise, in good faith, only to find when they received it that the goods were either seconds or damaged beyond repair. Consequently they could not be used or sold. A friend of mine purchased a large number of what he thought were top-of-the-line porcelain bathroom fixtures. What was finally delivered was a load of factory seconds - chipped and broken sinks, toilets, and baths, all of which were useless. When he sought retribution from the company he learned it was a fly-by-night operation which no longer existed. A second friend entered into a joint venture with a group of expatriates. He provided the capital for the company and the expatriates provided the know-how. He told me later that after four years of work they ended up with all the capital and he ended up with the know-how but no profits to show for his pains.

Another local merchant was persuaded to open a letter of credit against the importation of olives - 300 tons of olives - from an Arab country. At the time the consumption of olives in the whole UAE could not have exceeded ten tons yearly. His plan was to sell the olives throughout the Gulf region and the Middle East as he had been promised marketing assistance by the supplier with whom he had entered into a joint venture. The olives arrived in good condition. Unfortunately the agreed marketing support never materialised so they sat at the port for months.

I personally suffered a few similar incidents. I wrote up an agreement with a contractor to build some houses, paying him a substantial sum of money in advance to mobilise the equipment he needed to start the work. My mistake was not to ask him to provide a bank guarantee or a bid bond. He collected the money from me, and from several other businessmen with whom he had signed similar agreements, then fled the country with the cash, never to fulfill his part of the bargain.

In another case the wife of an imprisoned contractor begged me to help her husband. He had landed in jail for debt and had no way to defend himself or repay what he owed. Although I knew these people socially I had never had business dealings with them. They seemed in such distress, however, so genuine about making good on their loans that I decided to help them if I could. They asked me to give a bank guarantee to the court so the imprisoned contractor could be freed to defend himself. Once I had done so the contractor was released. He went straight from the prison to the airport – I never saw him or his wife again. Their way of thanking me for my help was to leave me liable for all the debts he had incurred.

This was the way it went in those days. We were inexperienced and tended to trust people implicitly whether we knew them or not. We believed everyone's intentions were honourable and that they would fulfil their promises as we did. That was how we had been brought up so we thought everyone else had been too. We entered into joint ventures in good faith, but instead of profits, many of us ended up with a mountain of debt while the expatriates fled the country with pockets full of cash.

Dozens of such situations befell my countrymen. Naive local merchants and businessmen, taken in by con men, lost hundreds of thousands of dirhams. I was a member of the board at the Chamber of Commerce so I witnessed the financial bloodbath first-hand. We eventually came to believe that most of those who said they wanted to do business were more interested in taking advantage of us in one way or another. We found out that no one could be trusted. It seemed that every carpetbagger and opportunist had heard of the easy money just waiting to be taken from unsuspecting entrepreneurs in the United Arab Emirates. We had to open our eyes before we were taken for everything we had. Thank God we learned quickly from our mistakes. The business community became more cautious. The federal government helped by laying down rules and regulations to protect us from such abuses and stem the financial stresses caused by dishonest people siphoning cash from our economy.

Thanks to the education we have since received, both from personal experience as well as formal schooling, we are no longer as naive as we once were. We are truly grateful for the funding that has been provided for education and the world of opportunities that has become available to us because of it. Had we had in the 1930s, 1940s and 1950s even a fraction of the education that is now being provided by our ministries and educational institutions we could have coped far better in those early years of development. We would have saved ourselves a lot of money, resources, and aggravation as well as the heartache and embarrassment of being the unwitting victims of unscrupulous businessmen and con artists. God knows how many such incidents we suffered. Only those who fell victim, many of whom would have been too embarrassed to admit it, know the true extent of the losses. Unfortunately these things happen in a developing economy though it took us some time to recognise the problem and put a stop to it. But we got through it all with our sense of humour, if not our pride, intact. Now we can look back, smile and say to ourselves "easy come, easy go".

Until the mid-1970s the economy was so healthy it could sustain these losses relatively painlessly. Unfortunately, the unprecedented prosperity was to be quite short lived.

From boom to bust

In the early stages of our struggle for recognition and acceptance by the world community, scarcely anyone, including nearby neighbours, was willing to befriend us without some kind of incentive. The demand on Sheikh Zayed to assist the less fortunate, less developed countries was tremendous. A large slice of the federal budget was set aside for a fund to help our neighbours - African, Arab and Muslim countries who required financial help - with various projects and programmes they wished to undertake. The establishment of the fund, called the Abu Dhabi Development Fund, opened the door for communication with these countries. Its purpose was two-fold. Using the fund as a vehicle, Sheikh Zayed helped needy countries with a great many development projects including electrification, roads, housing, mosques and schools. However, he also employed it as a diplomatic tool to persuade other countries to recognise the UAE as an independent state. Though his motivation may have been partly political, Sheikh Zayed never turned down a request for assistance. His reputation for almost overwhelming benevolence soon spread beyond our borders as he responded to each and every country seeking his support.

A steady stream of heads of state, foreign ministers, diplomats and assorted government officials was soon flowing to Sheikh Zayed's door. Some had never heard of us before, but the news of readily available financial assistance travelled quickly, so they began visiting the UAE to see the newly created country, and its beneficent ruler, for themselves. Many took advantage of Sheikh Zayed's seemingly unlimited generosity, particularly those in close proximity to our small state. They looked to us for financial assistance and support in a diversity of areas. All they had to do was come for a visit and ask for help; Sheikh Zayed invariably gave them money to finance projects and development schemes in their own countries. Sometimes it seemed we were assisting in every disaster and major project that was happening in the Arab world and neighbouring regions at the time.

We built roads and housing in Egypt; supported agricultural projects in Sudan; constructed race courses in Morocco; put up local housing in Pakistan; assisted the Somalis with various projects; built dams in Yemen; supported the Palestinians and the Jordanians; and we helped build medical clinics and schools all over – wherever we turned there was an outstretched hand. Naturally those funds were then not available for us to develop the UAE. It was challenging trying to build our own country with the resources we had, spreading ourselves so thin made it even more so. But we needed the goodwill and support of our neighbours and Arab brothers so we had no choice but to come to their aid when they were in need. Most of those we helped were gracious and appreciative of Sheikh Zayed's efforts but some went beyond the bounds of good manners.

We once had a head of state who stopped over in Abu Dhabi on his way back to his home country from Saudi Arabia. He stayed in Abu Dhabi for one day. As we were seeing him off at the airport after his visit, he turned to Sheikh Zayed and asked "Where is my cheque?" The diplomatic entourage was taken aback at his presumptuousness. He was told that his request for assistance would be reviewed and considered by the proper authorities. His response to that was even more surprising than his original request. "No, I expect to be paid immediately, I cannot wait for this to happen, I need the money now," he said boldly. We were all held up at the airport for close to an hour while this head of state negotiated with Sheikh Zayed for a handout. He agreed to board the aircraft only when he was promised a donation. Since no one writes cheques standing on an airport tarmac, however, he had one of his ministers removed from the plane to stay in Abu Dhabi while the appropriate paperwork was prepared. The minister was instructed to return home only with a cheque from Sheikh Zayed in hand!

When the oil revenues began to flow, it seemed everyone forgot that five years earlier we had been a virtually unknown people, without even a country, whom no one cared about or came to help. Yet here we were, with our new-found wealth, supporting nations near and far in the name of humanity, friendly relations and charity.

By 1976 the well had run dry. The demand on our financial resources was much greater than even our vast oil wealth could sustain. We found ourselves out of money and in a recession, from boom to bust in a matter of only a few short years. Of course we had never experienced anything like a recession before. Businesses were left with their goods stranded at the port or the airport because there were no funds available to clear them through customs. Major projects were left unfinished because of a lack of capital. Many people took the recession very personally. They were ashamed because they were unable to pay their debts and fulfil their promises; they felt that they had lost face with those who trusted them. Some were so desperately depressed about not being able to meet their commitments that they took their own lives.

Despite the economic slowdown, however, we continued to make significant progress in overcoming obstacles and implementing worthwhile initiatives in a number of key areas such as housing development.

Just as I had observed several years earlier, the government also recognised that the system of land gifts was not working as well as it might have. To resolve the situation, a special committee – called Sheikh Khalifa's Committee – was created in 1976 to administer the lands of people who could not adequately manage the holdings themselves. Five years later, in 1981, the committee became a fully-fledged government department – the Department of Buildings and Social Affairs. Essentially the government used the same strategy I had with the eighteen landowners, but did it on a much larger scale. It took over the management of local land holdings from beginning to end including building, then leasing out houses on each of the properties. At first, the rental proceeds were split, two-thirds went to the government to cover building and administrative costs, the remaining one-third was given to the property owner. Once the construction costs were paid, however, the full rental income was remitted to the landlord. This was a godsend to many. It saved them from having to sell their land and gave them a regular income.

Today, the same department builds and supervises thousands of rental properties on behalf of local landowners. This innovative programme, subsidised by the local government, is unique to Abu Dhabi – the only government agency worldwide, I believe, which provides services of this type. It awards parcels of land; designs, builds and leases housing on them; and administers the whole process for the landowners. All of this is offered absolutely free of charge. In addition to this service the department also provides Abu Dhabians with low-cost financing, at the unheard of rate of one half of one per cent yearly, to build housing and commercial buildings. Like Etisalat, the department is envied throughout the Arab world. The interest rate is incredibly low and there are no set time limits for the repayment of the loans; penalties are never levied no matter how slowly or how quickly the loans are repaid. This government assistance, a huge advantage for all property and landowners in Abu Dhabi, is in place thanks to the generosity of Sheikh Zayed and Sheikh Khalifa.

These types of programme kept us going through the recession which lasted for over two and a half years. We did not fully recover from the downturn until the latter part of 1980, when, in September, the Iran-Iraq war broke out thus forcing up oil prices on world markets.

When Abu Dhabi began to prosper as a result, Sheikh Zayed once again demonstrated his boundless generosity to his people. Feeling that Abu Dhabians had suffered more than their fair share during the recession, he devised a plan for once again redistributing the oil wealth throughout the emirate. He decreed that all those who had lost their homes because of development and town planning during the late 1960s should be compensated ten times the amount that they had originally received. This injected roughly two billion dirhams into Abu Dhabi's economy, helping lift the emirate, as well as the entire country, out of the recessionary crisis. The compensation jump-started the economy spurring on development in a more rational and logical fashion than the haphazard way that it had proceeded in the late 1960s and early 1970s.

Chapter 8

Shifting Sands

Money problems

The compensation scheme of the late 1970s played a central role in lifting our economy out of the doldrums and helping many recession battered businessmen repay their debts. However, as with other programmes which were of great benefit to many, this one too had some unexpected, and not entirely positive, results.

Having lived simply for so many years Abu Dhabians were unable to cope with the rate, degree and amount of change we were experiencing. Even the transition from poverty to sudden wealth was problematic. When they were given large sums of money many local people had no idea what to do with it, especially since it is forbidden by Islam to deposit money in the bank to earn interest. They had to do something, either invest it or spend it. Since most knew nothing about investing, many went on buying sprees purchasing big ticket items for which they had little need. This is exactly what happened when Sheikh Zayed decided to compensate Abu Dhabians for property which had been expropriated for town planning purposes between 1966 and 1968. People had received a goodly sum when their small plots of land were first turned over to the government. A decade later, however, as the Emirate and the rest of the country emerged from a three-year-long recession, Sheikh Zayed felt they deserved additional funds to help get them on their feet again. As part of the second compensation scheme of 1979 and 1980, many local inhabitants were paid hundreds of thousands, even millions, of dirhams. A substantial portion of the money was well spent by the recipients. But, just as had happened with the first compensation programme, some unfortunates were soon parted from their windfall either through bad luck or poor investments.

An acquaintance of mine decided to go into the taxi business with the funds he had been awarded through the re-compensation programme. He bought ten Toyota saloon cars to start his fleet and hired an equal number of drivers without knowing much more than their names. Before he knew it the drivers had all absconded with the brand new cars! He had not bothered to record the registration numbers of the vehicles, nor did he have any way to trace the missing men. His fleet was reduced from ten vehicles to none and he never saw any of his former employees again. He lost all the money he had been given by the government in one fell swoop.

Some people bought large homes and furnished them lavishly only to find they could not afford the maintenance costs on the new residences. Others bought transport and trucking companies thinking they could be easily managed, but their limited knowledge was not enough to keep the business running smoothly; many ended up losing everything they had. Inexperience in handling money was everyone's downfall. To save them from their own folly, Sheikh Zayed and the government took measures which safeguarded people from financial ruin. Local government rules and regulations were put in place to protect us as we learned to make sound financial decisions, both in our personal lives and in our business ventures. The UAE Central Bank, for example, passed a ruling limiting the amount banks could lend on personal loans; the loans could not exceed a quarter of a million dirhams. Also, bank guarantees were not easily obtained unless they were supported by funds and secured by contracts. Such measures were still being implemented as recently as 1988 when the government passed a ruling prohibiting banks from taking possession of properties against loans which borrowers were unable to repay.

Throughout the 1970s and 1980s, banks had accepted land, homes and commercial buildings as collateral against loans. When inexperienced local entrepreneurs failed in business ventures and defaulted on their loans, the banks often repossessed homes and properties in place of repayment. This meant that some Abu Dhabians found themselves in the street with nothing - no business, no income, no support and nowhere to live. Now that they have less collateral, the banks are much more cautious about who they lend money to and for what reason. At the same time, those who could lose everything if their business turns sour will at least have a roof over their heads. Both the banks and the entrepreneurs learned valuable lessons: the former scrutinise loan applications more carefully; the latter tend to be less eager to jump into risky business ventures at the drop of a hat.

During the late 1970s a new investment concept caught on in the UAE. A number of people would band together to form a company in one of the emirates then persuade the ruler of that emirate to pass a decree sanctioning the company. Once that was done they sold a certain percentage of the shares to the general public. The founding members - usually a combination of Kuwaiti, Bahraini and Emirati businessmen - would retain between twenty and forty per cent of the shares and offer the balance on the open market. The companies were set up to do business in various sectors including real estate, construction, livestock, food processing, banking, and imports-exports. The northern emirates were eager to participate in any effort to improve their economies and saw these new companies as a way to reach their growth objectives. Therefore, most of the ventures were set up in Umm al Qaiwain, Ras al Khaimah, Sharjah, and Ajman; a few were Dubai-based. There were none in Abu Dhabi as the Ruler would not pass decrees sanctioning such companies.

The companies' shares, which were traded on the Kuwaiti stock exchange, called Al Manakh, were handled by a number of UAE-based brokers. Initially they sold for relatively low prices – around ten dirhams per share. A lot of futures-type trading of the shares took place here in the Emirates; payments were made by post-dated cheques payable one year from the purchase date.

All this would have been well and good except a majority of these so-called businesses, which were supposed to be involved in real estate, banking, and the like, were in fact doing nothing more than trading their own shares on the stock exchange. Of course each of them had a board of directors or a management team, but these people did not run anything, they simply sat back, said they were in business and collected money as the share prices rose. The information about the organisations themselves was often very sketchy, all we heard was that their share prices kept increasing as people clamoured to jump on the get-rich-quick band wagon. The shares passed from one hand to the next and each time a transaction was made the price went up. Unfortunately there was no foundation for the price increases, no business behind the share certificates, no justification for the rapid inflation in their value.

This went on for five or six years until one fateful day in 1982 when some cheques bounced, the whole scheme fell to pieces and the Kuwaiti stock exchange collapsed. Many unhappy investors lost all their savings as a result – estimates suggested that 450 million dirhams was lost in the UAE alone. The loss of that huge amount of cash, which had been siphoned off from the Emirates over several years, was devastating to our economy. Many people had borrowed money from the banks to buy shares; they were left with nothing. This retarded economic growth, delayed development in some sectors and led to the financial ruin of many individuals, particularly in the northern emirates where the companies had been based. Like other set-backs, however, the catastrophic Kuwaiti stock market crash taught people a lesson they still remember. They became more cautious and took greater care to ensure there was some substance to the companies in which they planned to invest.

Many happy returns

As this sad tale unfolded around us the Al Fahim Group continued to prosper. In the late 1970s we entered into a joint venture with the world-renowned Holiday Inn chain of four-star hotels. The agreement was one that I, as managing director of our group of companies, had been considering for several years, but until then had resisted for various reasons. In the late 1970s Holiday Inn made me an offer I could not refuse. They would help me design and build the hotel, but they also offered to assist in forming a syndicate to finance its construction. All I had to do was accept the terms and conditions for the formation of the syndicate, including the interest rate. I finally agreed in 1979. The syndicate was formed. Its management was undertaken by the Abu Dhabi Investment Company (ADIC). We secured a loan for approximately twenty million dollars and construction began shortly thereafter on a piece of land our company owned on Sheikh Zayed the First Street. By 1982, the hotel – the first Holiday Inn in Abu Dhabi – was finished and ready for business. We capitalised on the increased influx of people resulting from the expansion of the oil industry and the related growth of the economy. Business flourished. It was so good in fact, that we decided to build a second property – The Corniche Residence – the management of which was subsequently awarded to the Hilton Group.

In the same year the Al Fahim Group decided to proceed with the Holiday Inn, war broke out between Iran and Iraq. While this negatively affected business in other Gulf countries it was a boon to the UAE. Being relatively distant from the centre of combat, we were viewed as a neutral country by the warring parties, both of whom relied on our strategic position for the supply of basic necessities such as food. The ports of the UAE were big enough to handle the volume of goods they required. So instead of receiving goods in their own respective ports – which was impossible because the shipping companies feared losing their vessels in the midst of the hostilities – both Iran and Iraq depended on ours. Most of the goods were off-loaded in Dubai or Jebel Ali and then transported either in small ferry boats or other vessels across the Gulf to Iran or overland by truck to Iraq in the north.

Instead of jeopardising business here, the war benefited our economy by increasing the volume of goods passing through our ports and boosting the demand for various products supplied by our merchants. In addition, many oil companies and large corporations operating in Iran, who either would not, or could not, be in the country while the war was on, set up shop in the UAE to maintain contact with their clients. They continued to supply them, from here, with fast moving consumers goods and basic necessities. The additional activity contributed to the growth of our economy throughout the 1980s.

Surprisingly, tourism also increased in the Emirates during that period, another reason why the country as a whole was keen to expand related facilities, including hotels, across the UAE generally and in Abu Dhabi in particular. Tourism was a welcome industry in Abu Dhabi: it helped diversify and strengthen an economy which was, and still is, so dependent on the oil industry. Tourism also gave us the opportunity to show the outside world how much we had achieved in the few short years since development had begun. The UAE has a lot to offer visitors: historical and archaeological sites, a unique culture, a temperate winter climate, fabulous desert scenery, crystal clear waters, rugged mountainscapes, cosmopolitan cities, exciting shopping venues and fine ethnic cuisines from around the world. All these natural wonders and man-made amenities entice visitors from everywhere to come to see our country and our accomplishments. To help accommodate visitors the local Abu Dhabi government established rest houses throughout the emirate.

While the Iran-Iraq war and the growing tourist trade contributed to our growth, the expansion of the oil industry in Abu Dhabi was also at a zenith in the 1980s. The oil companies, including all the ADNOC Group of Companies, tried wherever possible to involve local merchants and businessmen, helping them profit from the growth. They invited local businesses to participate in the tendering process and, whenever possible, they tried to meet their procurement needs locally. They studied tenders thoroughly, ensuring that local companies were neither overpaid nor underpaid for their services, while they diligently balanced costs against the value of services rendered. They advised the local businessmen of potential pitfalls, guiding many of them through the tendering process so that both purchaser and supplier were satisfied with the final results. The oil companies relied on the local businessmen to supply them with the highest quality products and services available on the market. They knew they could depend on them to be honest in their dealings. The local businessmen, on the other hand, trusted the oil companies to be fair. The tender process frequently resulted in locally-based ventures being called upon to supply goods, such as pipes and valves, or services, such as heavy equipment leasing.

The client-supplier relationship was excellent. As time went on, modest short-term financial gains eventually grew into more substantial long-term profits for the local suppliers. In some cases the oil companies might have been able to procure similar services from abroad, but instead they chose a local concern whenever possible. This strong and mutually beneficial relationship between the oil companies and the local business community remains intact today. It is one of the pillars of our successful economy and, I believe, unique to Abu Dhabi. The oil companies still go out of their way to involve locals whenever they can; the businessmen do their part by continuing to provide the quality, reliability and service upon which their customers have come to depend.

Opportunity knocks

1988 was a particularly bullish year for the economy in the United Arab Emirates, especially the Emirate of Abu Dhabi. There was considerable liquidity in the market, businesses were expanding, and a major reconstruction initiative started by the government around 1982 was in full swing. The Abu Dhabi Social Services and Buildings Department was demolishing and rebuilding many houses and commercial buildings which had been put up in the late 1960s and early 1970s. During those early stages of development both the design and construction of the buildings had been inferior. Brackish water had sometimes been used to make the cement and some foundations had been put in without sufficient pilings for the height of the building they were to support. This government-sponsored reconstruction continues to this day, but it was at a peak in the late 1980s. Since government spending fuels Abu Dhabi's growth to a great extent, prospects at the time were very promising.

A group of prominent Abu Dhabians decided to capitalise on the optimistic outlook by establishing a financial company that would deal in money management, currency trading and various other investments. There was no such company in Abu Dhabi at the time, most expatriates with money to invest were doing so with overseas money management companies and banks. This group of entrepreneurs felt they could better serve the Abu Dhabi market with an Abu Dhabi-based financial services company that would assist expatriates, as well as UAE nationals, who wished to invest in local ventures and overseas markets in New York, London, Hong Kong and Tokyo. Investors could then take advantage of the strong local economy while participating in overseas markets if and when they wished. The new organisation would be locally owned, funded and managed. It would provide a range of investment products and services easily, conveniently and cost-effectively, while precluding the necessity for frequent contact with overseas financial consultants.

Shortly after the company - the National Investment Security Corporation, or NISCORP - was created in March 1988, I was approached by Sheikh Saroor bin Sultan Al Dhahari, one of its founding members and chairman of the Abu Dhabi Commercial Bank, to invest as a shareholder. The founding members had already met three or four times, formed a board of directors, leased premises, obtained a licence from the Central Bank and received permission from the authorities to establish the company. I felt I should participate since it was a local venture and the first of its kind in Abu Dhabi. I wanted to encourage and support the group as well as the idea which I thought had considerable merit. Expatriates were not allowed to buy shares, own land or establish businesses without a local partner but many of them had substantial savings available for investment. Much of their money however, was generating only minimal returns on deposit with local and foreign banks. No one else had thought to assist the expatriate population with their investment needs; there was an excellent opportunity to provide a new service and make a profit doing so. Creating a company to help expatriates find local and international investments which would provide them with higher returns was, in my opinion, a useful undertaking. So I agreed to become involved.

When I attended my first meeting of the board of directors I discovered they had not yet nominated a chairman. Much to my surprise I found myself being proposed and supported as a candidate for the chair, despite the fact that it was my first meeting with the board. I declined at first but by the end of the meeting was convinced by the group of six directors that I should donate a portion of my time to making the company a success. We all agreed that once the business was firmly established, in two to three years, I would nominate someone else to take over. Under these conditions, and with the intent of contributing to an effort which I felt would be of benefit to Abu Dhabi, I accepted the chairmanship of NISCORP.

We met regularly, working hard to establish systems, set limits, contact foreign financial institutions, open accounts, propose ideas, implement business strategies and generally get things up and running. The first nine months went extraordinarily well. By the end of 1988 we were well underway with a good reputation and a name that was becoming known in the market. We opened several departments within the company, each handling a specific area of investment; while one dealt exclusively in the shares of local companies, for example, another was devoted to portfolio management, and so on. We had a strong response from investors as well as from the local banks who were willing to work with us by giving us credit facilities and opening accounts. We even had a daily report on local share prices and currency exchange rates published in one of the local Arabic newspapers; the report was widely read by bankers and members of the business community.

We had people from all nationalities involved in running the company: the managing director was an Abu Dhabian, the financial controller was Pakistani, the internal auditor Jordanian. We had a British marketing manager, an American real estate advisor, and other skilled professionals of differing backgrounds in various positions within the company which employed about sixty-five people.

A shooting star

In the first nine months of operation we made an excellent profit: around 7 million dirhams – a return of 17½ per cent on the original capital of 40 million dirhams with which we had started. This was a remarkable performance in less than a year – most companies do not even expect to break even, let alone make a profit, after their first year of operation. The second year, 1989, was even better and we anticipated a profit in the neighbourhood of 13 million dirhams. It was a good year for investments and, to meet the needs of our clients, we established several different funds, including a real estate fund and a currency fund. The latter, as the name suggests, was based on buying and selling foreign currencies on world money markets. Outside investors were invited to deposit a certain amount in the fund, the total monies deposited were then used to buy and sell the currencies. The fund profits, which we hoped to make over time, would be divided between all the investors. NISCORP did not own the fund but participated in it like all the other investors. The company's initial investment in the currency fund was 5 million dirhams, about 50 per cent of the total amount in the fund at the outset.

All our products and services, including the currency fund, proved very popular. The company was highly regarded by local investors and bankers alike because of the great strides we had made in such a short time. The funds were fairly large in view of the limited life span of the enterprise. People trusted the company and the board of directors: all were well-known, well-respected, prominent businessmen each of whom had his own successful businesses. The future seemed very bright indeed. In fact we were doing so well that we planned to acquire a local bank.

We had identified a need to add banking services to the range of financial products we offered and had approached a foreign bank who was interested in selling their UAE-based facilities to us. We met with them, established the terms and conditions, then put the proposal to the board where it was accepted. Once board approval for the acquisition was secured, we began to increase the capital of the company in order to finance the purchase of the banking operation which comprised two branches, one in Abu Dhabi and one in Dubai. Additional capital of 40 million dirhams was required for the purchase, thereby doubling the original capital used to set up NISCORP.

By the end of 1989 we were ready to expand our operations to encompass banking as well as investment services. We had laid down all the required rules and regulations and created a committee to supervise the takeover of the bank. All we needed to complete the deal was permission from the United Arab Emirates Central Bank. Unfortunately the Central Bank took a long time to study our application which had been submitted sometime in November. In the meantime, a new year dawned. Since financial businesses do not normally complete acquisitions or make large expenditures at the beginning of the year because of accounting considerations, the bank takeover was put on the back burner. In any case, most of the board members were out of town on other business at the beginning of the year so we did not meet until February. The Central Bank had still not approved our application, nor would it ever, in fact, give permission for the purchase, although we did not know that then.

As we pursued permission for the acquisition, another proposal was made – to establish a satellite office in Singapore to handle the company's investments in the Far East. Because of the time difference, we would be able to handle investments in Tokyo and Sydney much earlier from a Singapore-based office than was possible from Abu Dhabi. This would be advantageous to the company as well as to its shareholders and investors. NISCORP management's reports to the board were favourable, a profit of thirteen million dirhams was being projected for 1989. On the basis of the glowing reports we were receiving from the company's management, the board decided to proceed with the Singapore office. We sent one of the Abu Dhabi managers there to set up the operation, which he did over the following weeks.

Close call!

In March 1990, I travelled to Cyprus in my capacity as Vice President of the Abu Dhabi Chamber of Commerce. I returned from the trip via Dubai, picked up my car at the airport and set out for Abu Dhabi at about 10:00 p.m. There was a detour for some construction on the outskirts of Dubai, near the Metropolitan Hotel where the road was being widened. The road curved left before straightening once again after the construction zone. I must have dozed off, tired by a combination of lack of sleep, jet lag, the late hour and the motion of the vehicle. The last thing I remember is driving past the Trade Centre. When I came to the detour, the car, with me asleep at the wheel, continued to go straight instead of following the road which veered to the left. The car flipped end over end several times before coming to rest amidst the construction and sand.

A fellow Abu Dhabian driving behind me, who had recognised my vehicle by its licence plate number, was surprised by what had happened because I was not speeding and we were still within the city limits. He stopped to assist me though I did not know him personally. Apparently he helped me gather the contents of my briefcase which had been strewn all over the car during the accident. The next thing I recall is waking up in the hospital with my family gathered around my bed. Thanks to God and the seat belt I was not seriously injured, but the car was a total write-off. I still suffer from a bad shoulder as a result of the accident but it is a minor irritation in view of the severity of the damage that might have been done. Within a few days I was taken back to Abu Dhabi to recuperate from the accident at home.

While I was recovering, the managing director of NISCORP paid me a visit to tell me the Singapore office was ready to be officially opened. By that time I was well enough to travel again. Three of us, the managing director, myself and another member of the board, Anis Al Jallaf, flew to Singapore to inaugurate the office. The opening cocktail reception was attended by many prominent members of the Singaporean business, banking and financial community. The successful establishment of this branch office was a remarkable accomplishment for an Abu Dhabi-based company and we were justifiably proud of the achievement.

When we returned to Abu Dhabi the board was waiting for the company management to produce the 1989 year-end results and report so we could announce the profits and distribute the dividends to the shareholders. The senior managers told us the results still required the auditor's scrutiny and stamp of approval before they could be presented to the shareholders, but there was no reason to believe that this was anything more than a formality.

On 17 April the managing director and Anis Al Jallaf came to my office. Anis told me the managing director had something requiring my approval as chairman of the board. The managing director went on to explain that, while dealing in the currency fund, 2 million dirhams had been lost. He suggested to me that the company should make up this loss to the investors in order to maintain our strong position in the marketplace. While 2 million dirhams is a lot of money, it was not a great deal relative to the large sums in which we were dealing. Therefore I was ready to approve the managing director's request. However, the financial business was new to me and I wanted to make sure I had all the facts before I took a decision. I asked the managing director to write me a letter explaining how the money had been lost, confirming the exact amount of the loss and outlining how it would be replaced. He complied by drafting a letter assuring me the money would be recouped and restored to the currency fund within three weeks.

When, after the three weeks, I had not heard from the managing director, I conferred with the vice chairman of the board, Faraj bin Hamouda, telling him the information I had been given by the managing director. The vice chairman insisted we should hire independent auditors to look into the account to see whether the loss was the result of mismanagement or whether it was simply due to the vagaries of the currency markets. In May 1990 we hired Touche Ross, an internationally known and highly reputable company, to look into the business. A month later they warned us that the 2 million dirham figure we had been given was inaccurate. The actual loss exceeded this amount, they said, although they did not provide us with an updated estimate of the actual loss. We agreed to wait for the presentation of their formal report which would take another month to prepare. The report was finished on 6 August and given to the managing director. However, most of the board members were out of town at the time so it was not formally reviewed until the board met during the first week of September.

Shocking truths

In the meantime, Iraq had invaded Kuwait on 2 August. The sudden invasion sent a ripple of fear throughout the Gulf and, within a couple of weeks, caused a run on the company; many of NISCORP's investors wanted their money out immediately. The executive committee met at the end of August to decide how to deal with the run on the company. We were supported by many local banks and financial institutions and we believed we had sufficient credit to pay most of the investors.

When we saw the Touche Ross report about a week later, however, we were stunned to find the loss which had been incurred in the currency fund far exceeded 2 million dirhams. In fact, the amount was a staggering 160 million dirhams, twice that of the capital of the company and beyond anything we had anticipated as a worst-case scenario. We were utterly flabbergasted. In fact, we were so numb with shock we could hardly comprehend the situation let alone decide what to do about it. How could this have happened? The reports we had been given by the company management painted such a rosy outlook for NISCORP. How this financial disaster had come about was a total mystery to all of us on the board. Nevertheless, as we began to recover from the shock we tried our best to cut the company's losses.

We continued to meet through September in an effort to resolve the situation but each time we did so we were supplied with different figures by the managing director. By the end of 1990, as tensions in the Gulf continued to escalate, we fought our own battle trying to find ways to make up the huge losses. But the amounts were so staggering that we were unable to resolve the problem. At the shareholders' year-end meeting we proposed to turn the whole matter over to the Crown Prince's Court to decide how it should be dealt with. The Crown Prince's court, in its turn, referred the case to the legal system to find out what had happened, how it happened and who was responsible for the mess in which NISCORP found itself.

As chairman of the board, it seemed everyone - shareholders, investors, the courts, even other directors - turned to me for answers. But, like my fellow board members, I was completely in the dark with absolutely no knowledge of what had been happening or the extent of the losses until we saw the Touche Ross report in September 1990. Almost a year after the shock of seeing that report, we were all called to testify to the court during the the spring and summer of 1991. The court had appointed a special prosecutor to investigate the losses and how they had been incurred. By working diligently, questioning all who had been involved with the company, he eventually uncovered the truth. He found that the managing director, financial controller and internal auditor had collaborated to mislead the board, withhold information and falsify documents thereby incurring massive losses while concealing their activities from the board of directors and the shareholders. The three of them had colluded to cover up how the currency fund was being handled and the extent of the losses that were being incurred. It was through the investigations of the special prosecutor, who unravelled the mystery over a period of several months, that we eventually learned all the details.

Sometime in the autumn of 1989, unbeknown to the board of directors, the managing director had appointed someone outside the company to act as the dealer for the currency fund. This man worked out of his own home and was a personal friend of the managing director. He was unlawfully given control of the currency fund, as well as other monies including part of the capital of the company, by the managing director, acting without the knowledge or consent of the board. This situation continued until April 1990 when the man who was doing the trading died suddenly of a heart attack and the managing director came to me to advise me of the two million dirham loss. At that time neither I nor any of the other directors had any knowledge of the man. We knew nothing of the set-up in his home, his dealings with NISCORP's money, or the managing director's unauthorised transfer of the management of the currency fund to him. Of the many unlawful actions taken by the managing director, this last was probably the most brazen as the currency fund belonged to outside investors not NISCORP, the company itself having only a fifty per cent holding in the fund.

Furthermore, we found out that, from November 1989 onwards, the managing director, the financial controller and the internal auditor had misinformed the board of directors by setting up two sets of books, one which reflected the true position of the company - but which the board never saw - and a second, doctored to present a rosy financial picture, which was used to dupe the board members. Despite monthly meetings of the whole board and bi-weekly meetings of the executive, there was no way we could have known what was really happening because of the false information we were being fed by the three conspirators. While we thought everything was going well the company was actually sliding deeper into debt and financial ruin.

Even after the Touche Ross report, the managing director and his cronies kept on gambling and losing significant amounts of money in the markets. After NISCORP and its investors' money ran out, they borrowed from the banks, misleading them by falsifying loan applications, then taking the money they had borrowed and losing it on the currency markets. They never made a penny, they just kept gambling, losing and going deeper and deeper in the hole until the entire escapade ground to a halt when it was handed over to the courts.

The decision of the court was to send the culprits to prison, the managing director and the financial controller for three years and the internal auditor for two.

I then took over the company to dissolve it and liquidate the assets using the returns to repay some of the smaller portfolio holders and investors. The bank debts and the shareholders' losses were never repaid but there was nothing that could be done. The final liquidation of the company was completed by the special prosecutor in 1994.

While all the directors, myself included, were exonerated of any blame or wrongdoing, there was no avoiding some damage to the good reputations each of us had worked his whole life to build. This was a bitter pill to swallow, particularly as we had all become involved in the venture with the intention of building a business that would benefit investors while it strengthened the standing of Abu Dhabi as a centre of commerce and finance. Thank God we emerged from the crisis quite unscathed although the experience dampened our enthusiasm and made us wary of involving ourselves in new enterprises regardless of their apparent merit.

Of course all the board members suffered significant financial losses. But the losses were of little consequence compared with the injury to our reputations as honest, reliable and trustworthy businessmen. Our good names were our primary concern. A businessman's reputation is the foundation upon which his livelihood is built; this episode could easily have destroyed us all had the truth not been uncovered and the culprits exposed. Thankfully the people who were responsible were prosecuted and punished.

The whole affair left me deflated, wishing I had never become involved with NISCORP; although, there are always lessons to be gleaned no matter how dismal the situation. I learned to be doubly vigilant especially in dealings involving other people's money; I discovered how dishonest, deceitful and greedy some can be when it comes to handling finances; and, while NISCORP was only my first foray into the world of financial management companies, by the time the whole thing was over I had firmly resolved to make it my last.

Chapter 9

Beyond Our Dreams

Persistence pays off

While the NISCORP situation occupied a great deal of my time in the latter part of the 1980s, it did not monopolise it to the degree that I could not take steps forward on other fronts. In fact, as much as this was a time of disappointment because of NISCORP, it was also a period of great pride and achievement for both myself and the Al Fahim Group.

Having completed the Corniche Hotel in Abu Dhabi in 1982, we began to look at the potential for a similar venture in Dubai. As a first step, we bought a piece of land on the Al Maktoum Road. As soon as word got out that we had purchased the lot to build a hotel, the value of the adjacent land rose rapidly and we found ourselves in a position where it was far more attractive to sell the newly acquired plot at a substantial profit rather than go ahead with our construction plans. We looked at several other suitable sites but whenever we bought we found ourselves in a similar situation - unexpectedly making money in the real estate business instead of the hotel trade. Finally, in 1988 we purchased a small piece of land close to the Trade Centre on the Abu Dhabi - Dubai road. I felt it would be an excellent location for a hotel.

Unfortunately we found out later that the plot we had purchased was too small for the size of hotel that would be viable in that location. In addition, I had begun to envisage a project involving more than just a hotel, and my calculations indicated I would need more land for the larger scale development I had in mind. Once I had fleshed out the details I approached my father with the proposal; he was very receptive. Together we drafted a letter to Sheikh Maktoum, the Ruler of Dubai, outlining our thoughts on the project. Sheikh Maktoum was more than generous in response: he ordered that a piece of land twice the size of the one we already had be awarded to my father at no charge. The land was a very generous and much appreciated gift from Sheikh Maktoum to our family. Thus I found myself committed to a project comprising not only a hotel, but an office complex, a furnished apartment building, and a shopping centre as well. Naturally the banks were more than willing to participate in such a promising development. Once the financing was in place construction began.

The project took about five years to complete; we started in 1989 and finished in 1994. During that time Iraq invaded Kuwait causing a war which, it was feared, might spill over into neighbouring countries and perhaps even affect us directly in the Emirates. Because of that fear a flood of people transferred their savings out of the country. Many expatriates shut down their shops or businesses and fled to their countries of origin to sit out the conflict. Like most of my compatriots, I stayed, continued to work, and saw the period of instability through to its end without a thought of abandoning the projects we had underway. Despite the relative youth of our nation, the citizens of the United Arab Emirates are very patriotic, devoted to their country and willing to work hard to see it succeed. They believe, as I do, that our resources and monies should stay here in our own land, this is where we must invest our energies, both now and in the future. This is where we belong. The Gulf war was simply another obstacle to be overcome as we persisted in our development efforts.

Thanks to Sheikh Zayed's wisdom and decisiveness we had managed to steer clear of any regional conflicts until Saddam Hussein invaded Kuwait. When that happened we could no longer remain aloof as the UAE was on his list of possible targets. We had to defend ourselves though we could not understand why an Arab country, a Muslim country, would invade one of its neighbours. In any case, we condemned the aggression, along with our fellow members in the Gulf Cooperation Council, and, with the help of the West, the Americans and British in particular, the invasion was rebuffed. We all thank God the war was short-lived, contained within a small area in the northern part of the Gulf and concluded in favour of the Kuwaitis.

Despite the war and thanks to God's grace and the support of my family, the hotel was finally finished. At a time when everyone was very pessimistic and unsure of what the future held, we persisted. We believed strongly in what we were doing and committed our energies to seeing the project through. The Dubai Holiday Centre, which cost 465 million dirhams to build, was partially opened in the summer of 1994 and fully finished by the end of the same year. It hosted a major conference shortly afterwards and continues to do very well. Immediately upon its completion we received an offer of 1.2 billion dirhams for the property. We rejected it despite the fact that the offer was almost three times what it had cost to build the Centre and we could have used the capital to fund other projects or the expansion of other Al Fahim Group businesses.

The Dubai property is more than just another business holding for our Group. To us it is a symbol, evidence of what a local businessman can do, given the opportunity and the support. It is the culmination of five years of intense efforts spanning a period of war and uncertainty, evidence of our determination not to be deterred from our objectives no matter what the circumstances. It is testament to our belief that infusing capital into our own economy is more worthwhile than investing it in the banks of Europe and America. The Dubai Holiday Centre is an outstanding example of both the generosity of our Rulers, especially Sheikh Maktoum who donated part of the land on which it is built, and the Government of Dubai whose cooperation throughout the project made our job easier. The Dubai government gave us virtually unlimited support, even though the location was as yet un-serviced when the project began. When the hotel was finished, the local government departments connected us to all the required municipal services from electricity to sewage without extra charges or undue delays. Today we have a deluxe 650 room property serving not only the residents of Dubai but the whole region by welcoming guests, hosting important conferences, sponsoring special promotions and contributing to the overall health of the economy.

It is gratifying to see this achievement. More so because it is the result of hard work, dedication and a belief in our ability to do something important, to make a contribution to the growth of our economy and to the well-being of all who live in the Emirates. I believe every citizen in the UAE must participate in the development of our country, especially since we, the people of the Emirates, are so few in number. We are the minority in our own country. Nevertheless, we should be able to provide for the majority. In fact, it is our responsibility to do so. We are the hosts of all others who work in our country, helping us to move forward, build an infrastructure and expand our economy. We have a responsibility to those people and to ourselves. We must resist the temptation to siphon off cash from our businesses and move it abroad for safe keeping. We must believe in the UAE. It is our duty to maximise the use of all our resources, work together to realise the vision of our leaders and make this country an example for others to follow.

Faith, hope and perseverance
The Dubai Holiday Centre is but one of hundreds of success stories to be found in the United Arab Emirates. Our achievements over the past thirty years, both as individuals and as a nation, are astounding. The transformation resulting from our efforts has taken us from rags to riches in less than a generation.

The small fishing settlement which counted less than fifteen hundred souls in 1950, and only double that a little more than a decade later, is now a modern city with a population of over half a million people. We live in contemporary housing and high rise buildings instead of primitive huts made of palm fronds or mud. We have air conditioning to cool us in the intense heat of summer; blankets, jackets and sweaters to warm ourselves during the chill winter evenings. We no longer drink brackish water drawn from hand-dug wells and hauled to our homes in goat skins. We have fresh desalinated water piped directly wherever we need it, at considerable expense to the government but at almost no cost to us. We no longer wash in the sea. Instead we shower and bathe in the comfort of marbled and mirrored bathrooms that would be the envy of Roman emperors.

We have modern hospitals to care for the sick - children who might have been orphaned thirty years ago now grow up nurtured by their mother's love instead. We do not travel by camel caravan anymore, spending days on end to reach our desired destinations. Now we drive in supercharged, high-powered motorcars, capable of very fast speeds. What was once a seven-day journey from Abu Dhabi to Al Ain now takes less than two hours. The rough tracks that wound helter-skelter between our barasti huts and across the sand have been replaced by a well-planned road system used daily by tens of thousands of vehicles. The thoroughfares are numbered and named, lined with either brick sidewalks or lush flora that changes with the season. Our children are educated at private schools, both here and abroad; gone are the days of the ill-equipped schoolhouse with a single teacher.

We no longer need to rely on charity as we once had to in 1959 when Abu Dhabi was flooded and the British assisted us with donations of food and blankets. The tables have long since turned. Using our new found oil wealth, we now help others in need with aid such as food, shelter and medicines. Both individually and collectively we have assisted in scores of worthwhile projects all over the world including building schools, mosques, irrigation equipment, training facilities and low-cost housing. We have sent donations of food, blankets and other supplies to war-torn regions in Afghanistan, Somalia, Bosnia-Herzegovina and Chechnya. We are now in the privileged position of being able to help the disadvantaged and the down-trodden regardless of their race, colour or creed. Thank God for our good fortune.

We can afford to buy and do many things today that we only dreamed of yesterday. Many of us have money enough to travel almost anywhere, at any time; across the Middle East, to Asia and Europe, even as far as the Americas. The world is our oyster. God has been extraordinarily generous to us, for which we should always be thankful. As a nation, we have been more than compensated for what our people suffered before development finally got underway.

We are wealthier, healthier and much happier people in 1995 than we were less than three decades ago, although our new found wealth, health and happiness did not come easily. As a people, we had been patient, resilient and hopeful for a long time before we stepped tentatively, though proudly, into the twentieth century. Our faith in God sustained us through many long dark years, keeping alive our belief in a destiny which included prosperity for all. Despite the pain and deprivation we suffered we trusted there would be light at the end of the tunnel and we continued to seek that light. We spent days and nights, weeks and months, searching, hoping and praying for deliverance. Thank God deliverance finally found us, not lying idle in the shade of a palm tree, but working hard, striving in every way possible to improve our lot and realise our dreams.

Each of my compatriots had spent a lifetime working toward the day we would all be free of hardship: either sweating it out with shovels in the employ of the oil companies, spending endless hours on guard duty in the offshore oil installations, working for years on the islands for meagre financial rewards, travelling for months in the desert on camel-back, tending sheep or farming under the hot sun in the Liwa or Al Ain. As time went on anyone who was old enough to do so participated in turning Abu Dhabi around. It fell on our generation to fulfil the dreams of our forefathers. We persevered, trying every avenue to reach our goals. We laboured long and hard in meetings, reviewing plans and blueprints, seeking solutions to countless seemingly insoluble problems. We investigated promising opportunities, started up businesses, supervised projects, evaluated our work and sought better, more efficient ways to achieve our ends. It was never easy. Everything we see around us, from the street lights to the mirrored buildings, took a lot of creative thinking, hard work and perseverance.

Loyal to our country and resolute in believing in a better tomorrow, many of us resisted the temptation to emigrate to other countries, both near and far, though at the time prospects away may have seemed more attractive than those here at home. Abu Dhabians who had no choice but to leave eventually returned to support our efforts by sharing their acquired knowledge and know-how. But no matter what our circumstances, all of us, from every walk of life, worked together to form a strong, integrated community in the Emirate of Abu Dhabi, a community that makes a significant contribution to the health and well-being of our nation as a whole. And despite all our success we have not become complacent. We are continually looking for ways to improve our lives and make things even better for our children.

Over the past thirty years we have been very fortunate to have a ruler whose incredible vision was matched by a quiet determination to see our dreams become a reality. Sheikh Zayed bin Sultan Al Nahyan has provided us with more than just financial and moral support. He has been a beacon, leading us from the past into the future, never wavering in his devotion to his people, never giving up when all the odds seemed against him, never losing faith in the hours of darkness.

We are equally fortunate to have had a committed government to help us, steering us in the right direction, improving our livelihood by supporting us financially and making it not only possible, but easy, to earn a good living. Our system of government, which is socialistic in many respects, fosters an environment in which individuals are urged to contribute to efforts that will improve the welfare of all. The government encourages entrepreneurs by supporting those who combine their resources to form groups, cooperatives, or syndicates that in their turn develop, introduce or create new businesses and organisations that will ultimately benefit the society as a whole. Whether those businesses are in the service industry, manufacturing, banking, investment or trading, the government tends to favour joint ventures and partnerships between local businessmen, thus passing along the benefits of the oil revenues to as many people as possible. Individualism, on the other hand, is discouraged for its tendency to foster jealousy and envy. Entrepreneurs who work in isolation from others in the business community generally face an uphill battle in their endeavours. In Abu Dhabi the route to success is more likely to be paved with cooperation - people work together for the ultimate benefit of all citizens. Joint ventures and companies which have been formed with government support have an edge in the healthy competition for government contracts and tenders.

We owe a great deal to Sheikh Zayed for his unflagging support and to the local and federal governments for their encouragement. Still, it was the people of Abu Dhabi and the UAE who did the work that transformed our country into the success story it is today.

We faced and overcame countless obstacles along the way, many of which seemed insurmountable at the time. Nevertheless, those hurdles will soon seem insignificant compared with the challenges of the future, for it is far more difficult to maintain success over time than it is to achieve it in the first place. We are at the crossroads of tomorrow, even now as we bask in the glow of our recent accomplishments. We are well off both financially and socially, we have excellent medical care and social security, we have lifetime employment. Everything we need to live, even thrive, is being provided for us. It will be a challenge for the younger generation to take over where we leave off and to maintain this standard of living. Nevertheless, they must surpass our achievements if the country is to continue growing.

Our generation, and the one which preceded it, have laid the foundation for a bright future. However, as everyone knows, the only sure thing about tomorrow is that, God willing, the sun will continue to rise in the east and set in the west. Beyond that the future is in no way guaranteed. Our children and our children's children will have to work hard, using all the resources at their disposal to ensure the foundation we have built does not crumble beneath them. They must conserve what we have created, carry the torch further down the road of progress and ensure that our rags-to-riches story is told to future generations so they too understand the value of faith, hope and perseverance. They must learn to do things better and more cost-effectively than we have done. We made a lot of mistakes along the road to development, many of which cost us dearly. We hope and pray that those who follow in our footsteps will learn, as we did, from our mistakes, thus avoiding some of the pitfalls we encountered.

Education is the key
Of the many lessons we learned, two tower above all the others in importance. First and foremost is to have faith in God, without Him we are nothing. The second lesson is that education is one of the most powerful tools and important pillars of a flourishing nation: without it a society can wither and die. The little amount of education my contemporaries and I received was not enough, even for our time and place. Our children and their offspring will have more opportunities to pursue higher levels of education; I only hope they do not let those opportunities pass them by. I encourage them to reach out and grab every chance they get to equip themselves with the tools that only good schooling can give, tools that are being provided thanks to the commitment of men such as Sheikh Nahyan bin Mubarak Al Nahyan, Minister of Higher Education and President of Al Ain University.

From the day he assumed the Presidency of Al Ain University in 1982, Sheikh Nahyan has worked tirelessly, driven by his deep commitment to higher education and his belief that it will be the foundation for the future. He has spared neither expense nor effort in making the educational system in the UAE an example to be followed throughout the Gulf area. He has been one of the main players in the establishment of the higher colleges of technology which together have vastly improved the educational opportunities available to UAE nationals. Through his efforts and foresight he has made great contributions to the educational system. Sheikh Nahyan, however, must not be a one man show. Without the financial support of the government or the moral support of UAE citizens and parents, he will be unable to carry on with his invaluable work. It is crucial, therefore, that both the people of the UAE and the government continue to support efforts such as his. Education is simply vital for the ongoing growth and prosperity of our country.

Besides being the key to the future, education is the best way to preserve the past and document the present. Countless generations of our people have lived and died without a trace because there are no written records of their lives or achievements. Even the past 200 years remain undocumented for the most part, except for records and correspondence kept by the British and other colonial powers interested in our domination, not our development. Although our rich history goes back many centuries, only bits and pieces of the last several decades have been written by our own historians and scholars. We are in a lamentable position. We must study the past from the perspective of foreigners, using their old documents and photographs in our research. The past as seen through the eyes of our own ancestors is lost forever, simply because most of our fathers, and their fathers, could neither read nor write. We only began documenting the events of the day and recording our own history toward the latter part of the 1960s. Now that we have the tools to do so, we must continue to record the important events of our times so that others, including our children's children can benefit from our experiences. We must not become like some civilisations of the past which vanished without a trace mainly because nothing was written about them during their prime. Unlike these forgotten peoples, our people must not pass through history unnoticed. We have an opportunity to make our contributions count today and in the future.

Pursuing higher education will also allow us to participate more fully in the affairs of the Arab world, influencing policy and making a difference in the lives of people across the Middle East. It will ensure that we are able to preserve our independence and our way of life by becoming more meaningful contributors to the Gulf Cooperation Council. It is essential that we participate as intellectual equals in joint ventures such as these. Educating ourselves to the highest standards will enable us to meet the challenges associated with managing the relationships we have forged with countries and colleagues throughout the Middle East and around the world. We will become even more active and more influential members of the Arab community, participating to a greater extent in the negotiations and decision-making processes that affect the future of our country, the region and, ultimately, the world. In the past, although we have been part of the Arab community, we have been accepted because we have paid handsomely for the privilege of participating. In the future we must not simply be the "funding fathers" - our role must go far beyond that. We must be accepted for what we have to offer as equal partners in the decision-making process rather than simply the ones who provide the cash. Our leaders and scholars have a great deal to bring to the table, they should be accepted for their skills, wisdom and expertise rather than their ability to pay their way in. Education will help us to attain our rightful position.

For these reasons the efforts of ministers such as Sheikh Nahyan bin Mubarak and Hamad Al Madfaa to further the education of UAE nationals should be fully supported by each and every citizen of our country. No amount of infrastructure, from highways to high-rises or televisions to telecommunications, can ever equal the power of education. It is our responsibility to give the next generation the gift of learning so they can take our country beyond our dreams. We must also teach our children to live peacefully, in harmony with nature and their fellow human beings. Our society is now a cosmopolitan one in which people of all different races, colours and creeds work, study and play side by side. We must be respectful of others' beliefs and wishes, tolerant of different cultures and nationalities, more understanding of diversity.

Our government looks favourably on initiatives which involve groups of people working together in partnership to achieve goals and objectives. As UAE nationals it is our duty to live by the same ideals. We constitute the minority in our own country but it is our responsibility to earn the respect and gratitude of the majority, who are expatriates, by being welcoming hosts, forthright business partners, able competitors and fair employers. Foreign workers are guests in our country, here to perform a job or complete an assignment that will help us to continue to move forward. We must not set ourselves apart from those who work with us, or those who work for us, as everyone who lives here contributes in some way toward the betterment of our society. As good hosts we must treat them with patience, respect and kindness, creating an example for nations throughout the world by the way we conduct ourselves toward each other as well as to the expatriates in our country.

I have written this book in hope - hope that the efforts of my generation and the generations before us will not be in vain. Hope that our children, in knowing of the toil, sweat and tears we suffered to make their lives easier and their upbringing happier than our own, will take courage from our stories as they work at making the future even better for their own families. I pray they will maximise their educational opportunities, growing stronger as individuals and thereby strengthening the backbone of our nation. Our future is full of promise just waiting to be fulfilled, though it will take a lot of commitment and hard work to see our dreams realised. We have done our part. Now our children must take up the challenges of tomorrow's world, a world of computers and advanced technology operating at lightning speed in a global economy. As a country we have only one way to go: forward. I hope that our educational efforts will help the next generation see the path they should follow, to do better than we have done.

I also fervently hope that our federation will survive well into the future, united and strong. For almost thirty years we have lived under the protection of a wise and insightful leader, Sheikh Zayed bin Sultan Al Nahyan. While he lives and we are sheltered by his umbrella of security, we have no one to fear but God. When the day comes that this umbrella is lifted I pray that nothing will deter us from reaching the goals he has set for us. We must persist in the face of adversity, maintain the unity he worked for so long to achieve, take pride in our many accomplishments and rebuff any threat to the strength of our country for it is fundamental to our very survival and the security of future generations.

Glossary of Gulf terms

Arabic	English
abbaya	cloak
agal	headcloth–cord
anna	16 to the rupee
barasti	huts made of palm tree wood
dhub	lizard
dishdash	long, sleeved shirt-like man's garment
gutra	headcloth
kandoura	(as "dishdash")
majlis	a room for receiving guests
mulla	religious teacher
rupee	Indian coin
sabkha	salt-flat
shamal	strong wind from North
souk	bazaar